Managing

K-

Addison-Wesley Information Technology Series

Capers Jones, Series Editor

The information technology (IT) industry is in the public eye now more than ever before because of a number of major issues in which software technology and national policies are closely related. As the use of software expands, there is a continuing need for business and software professionals to stay current with the state of the art in software methodologies and technologies. The goal of the Addison-Wesley Information Technology Series is to cover any and all topics that affect the IT community: These books illustrate and explore how information technology can be aligned with business practices to achieve business goals and support business imperatives. Addison-Wesley has created this innovative series to empower you with the benefits of the industry experts' experience.

For more information point your browser to
http://www.awl.com/cseng/series/it/

Wayne Applehans, Alden Globe, and Greg Laugero, *Managing Knowledge: A Practical Web-Based Approach.*
ISBN: 0-201-43315-X

Gregory C. Dennis and James R. Rubin, *Mission-Critical Java™ Project Management: Business Strategies, Applications, and Development.*
ISBN: 0-201-32573-X

Kevin Dick, *XML: A Manager's Guide.*
ISBN: 0-201-43335-4

Capers Jones, *The Year 2000 Software Problem: Quantifying the Costs and Assessing the Consequences.* ISBN: 0-201-30964-5

Ravi Kalakota and Marcia Robinson, *e-Business: Roadmap for Success.*
ISBN: 0-201-60480-9

Sergio Lozinsky, *Enterprise-Wide Software Solutions: Integration Strategies and Practices.* ISBN: 0-201-30971-8

Patrick O'Beirne, *Managing the Euro in Information Systems: Strategies for Successful Changeover.* ISBN: 0-201-60482-5

Managing Knowledge

A Practical Web-Based Approach

Wayne Applehans
Alden Globe
Greg Laugero

ADDISON–WESLEY
An Imprint of Addison Wesley Longman, Inc.

Reading, Massachusetts • Harlow, England • Menlo Park, California
Berkeley, California • Don Mills, Ontario • Sydney
Bonn • Amsterdam • Tokyo • Mexico City

Many of the designations used by manufacturers and sellers to distinguish their products are claimed as trademarks. Where those designations appear in this book, and Addison Wesley Longman, Inc. was aware of a trademark claim, the designations have been printed in initial capital letters or all capital letters.

The authors and publisher have taken care in preparation of this book, but make no expressed or implied warranty of any kind and assume no responsibility for errors or omissions. No liability is assumed for incidental or consequential damages in connection with or arising out of the use of the information or programs contained herein.

The publisher offers discounts of this book when ordered in quantity for special sales. For more information, please contact:

AWL Direct Sales
Addison Wesley Longman, Inc.
One Jacob Way
Reading, Massachusetts 01867

£ 22.99

Visit Addison-Wesley on the Web: http://www.awl.com/cseng/

Library of Congress Cataloging-in-Publication Data

Applehans, Wayne.
    Managing knowledge : a practical web-based approach / Wayne Applehans, Alden Globe, Greg Laugero.
        p. cm.— (Addison-Wesley information technology series)
    Includes index.
    ISBN 0-201-43315-X
    1. Database management. 2. World Wide Web (Information retrieval system) 3. Information resources management. I. Globe, Alden. II. Laugero, Greg. III. Title. IV. Series.
    QA76.9.D3 A665 1999
    025.04—dc21
                                                        98-43437
                                                        CIP

Text printed on recycled and acid-free paper.

ISBN 020143315X

3 4 5 6 7 8 CRW 02 01 00 99

3rd Printing August 1999

Contents

Chapter Two: Profiling People 37

Whom Do You Profile? 37
How Do You Profile? 38

Part Two: Organizing Around Knowledge 43

Chapter Three: Storyboarding Knowledge 45

Mapping People and Content 45
Step One: Identifying Your Strategic Business Cycles 46
Step Two: Mapping Your Information Leverage Points 48
Step Three: Adding the People 50
Step Four: Identifying the Content 52

Chapter Four: Mapping the Knowledge Network 57

Step One: Identifying Content Centers 60
Step Two: Adding Content Satellites 62
Step Three: Staffing and Assigning Ownership 64

Part Three: Knowledge Architecture 67

Chapter Five: Hiring People 69

The Levels of Knowledge Managers 69
Knowledge Analyst 71
Knowledge Author 72
Extended Team 73

A man should keep his little brain attic stocked with all the furniture he is likely to use, and the rest he can put away in the lumber room of his library, where he can get it if he wants it.

—Sir Arthur Conan Doyle
The Five Orange Pips

Who Should Read This Book?

 Is your company saving millions of dollars by getting people the information they need?

 Are you sharing information effectively across time zones, cultures, and geographic boundaries?

 Do you have corporate standards for creating, capturing, and delivering important content?

> *Managing Knowledge is about picking a strategic place in your organization that can benefit from managing its knowledge and getting started.*

At the end of the 20th century, will your organization be among the shrinking number of companies who aren't *managing knowledge*? Many companies realize they need to do this, but they don't know how to begin. This book will help you get started with a *knowledge management* (KM) project. To that end, we focus on the practical application of concepts and techniques that have been useful to us in our efforts. We believe you can use these concepts and procedures in setting up and running your own Web-based KM initiative.

Is This Book Right for You?

This book is for those people who have read some or all of the academic literature on KM, and who (along with their bosses) are convinced that they need to go down this path. Hopefully, you have a champion and an understanding of your company's long-range plan (LRP). If not, you need to target someone and make them read *Working Knowledge* by Thomas H. Davenport and Laurence Prusak, *Intellectual Capital* by Thomas A. Stewart, and *The Knowledge-Creating Company* by Ikujiro Nonaka and Hirotaka Takeuchi, among the many other academic studies on this important topic. These are excellent discussions of the scope of KM, and they were some of the important early motivators for us.

But for those of you looking to get a project or initiative off the ground, this book can help. Maybe you've been formal-ly charged with looking into KM and coming back with some recommendations, but you're not sure where to start. Perhaps your company has a functioning Intranet or Extranet, but the content is out of date and no one seems to be taking the lead on keeping it "fresh." Maybe you have an Intranet with thousands of pages, but you constantly hear the complaint, "I can't find anything, and when I do, I don't know if it's accurate." If you are facing these circumstances, this book is for you.

Why This Book Is Different

While the academic literature on KM is essential reading, there are some important differences between *Managing Knowledge* and those earlier works. The difference is that those books are exceptionally good at convincing you that you *should* do KM, but we'll try to convince you that you *can* do it. Accordingly, we make some assumptions that may or may not be shared with these other works.

Assumption One: Knowledge management does not have to be "profound."

Our purpose is not to address the nature of knowledge. Rather, we want to help you get the right information to the right people so they can take effective action. In this sense, our definition of "managing knowledge" is much more modest than what you may have read elsewhere. It involves understanding who needs what content to be successful in their jobs. In this book, we give you the tools and techniques to make these determinations.

Assumption Two: You have a champion and are figuring out how to get started.

While it is necessary to "think big," you'll need to "start small." *Managing Knowledge* is about picking a strategic place in your organization that can benefit from managing its knowledge and getting started. In this sense, we aren't going to take on the whole concept of KM. In fact, we're not interested in trying to define the entire scope of this important emerging field. We leave that to others. Accordingly, we don't undertake "literature surveys" or try to delve into the history of knowledge in Western society.

Assumption Three: Document management concepts, technologies, and procedures provide the basic discipline to kick off a successful effort.

The document is an important concept for getting started. In most cases, documents are going to be the vehicles for knowledge. Whether we're talking about HTML pages with links to other documents, application presentation layers with a view into databases, e-mail messages, or multimedia presentations, your focus will be moving knowledge inside and outside your company using documents.

That said, document management provides the central framework and discipline for successfully capturing, validating, and moving content to employees, partners, and customers. We discuss in detail how to set up classification systems (a.k.a. metadata) and the importance of "tagging" documents with consistent classifications. Without these skills, even so-called collaborative technologies won't be as effective as they could be.

Assumption Four: Yours is a mid- to large-size company with an Intranet and Extranet, as well as an Internet presence.

Everything we say in this book assumes that you are (or are going to be) leveraging Web-based technologies to move data, information, and knowledge. While conference calls, digital whiteboards, and pen and paper are viable tools, we believe that the most efficient way to move information within a mid- to large-

While other books may have convinced you to DO KM, this book tells you HOW.

size company (1000 employees or more) is via an Intranet. We also assume that your company is willing to fund a KM effort. Smaller companies that are centrally located and "tight knit" may be able to move information using less sophisticated means. But if you're larger and globally dispersed—and especially if you have an extensive partnership network—you must have an Intranet/Extranet.

Assumption Five: Your business is consciously preparing for the information economy.

Your executives or boss or someone influential (maybe you) believes that your company must begin retooling itself for the *information economy*. You don't need convincing any longer. Rather, you want to get started so that you can reap the benefits of competitive advantage before these advantages dry up and become "me too" processes and "best business practices." We'll help you get started by providing a method for taking the oversized concept that is KM and breaking it down into digestible parts that you can implement in the near term. ◎

It began with the arrival of personal computers, open markets and globalization in the early 1980s.

—*Wired Magazine*

Acknowledgments

Much of the practical, hard-won knowledge that went into this book was the result of long hours spent between 1994 and 1998 developing solutions and approaches to worldwide, Web-based KM challenges at J.D. Edwards, a business software developer in Denver, Colorado. Thanks go to J.D. Edwards officers Ed McVaney, Chairman of the Board; Buffy Collison, senior vice president of worldwide marketing; and Gay Dickerson, director of media creators, for sharing our vision and helping lead the way.

Members of our Knowledge Resource Strategies Group who helped develop and refine the concepts presented in this book, and with whom it has been a great pleasure to work, include Kristen Schiffner, Bob Zasuly, Michael Lavker, Meredith Monticello, and Debbie Arellano. Special thanks also go to Laurie Fetterolf, J.D. Edwards information and interface designer extraordinaire, who in addition to refining many KM concepts at J.D. Edwards also designed this book. Eagle-eyed online editor K.P. Nelson has been a tremendous help. Many J.D. Edwards technologists deserve praise and credit here as well: Paul Orsak, founder of the Knowledge Garden, and those who helped get us off the ground, including our Internet Services Group and IT department under CIO Mark Endry, and our MIS director Gerry Coady. There are, of course, many other individuals too numerous to mention.

A tip of the hat goes to SkyWeb's Brian Ward. Thanks to Deb Blecha of Raymond James Consulting. Lee Butler, Sherri Philips, Henry Winkler, and Tulsi Dharmarajan of Microsoft Consulting Services Denver gave much of their time, effort, and support. Thanks to Susan Kannel and Betty Konarski at the Office of Corporate Education at Regis University in Denver. Thanks to Alexis de Planque, senior consultant of Meta Group. Thanks to Denise Vega and Chris Katsaropoulos for paving the path for first-time authors. Thank you to the residents of Steamboat Springs, Colorado for openness to new ideas, friendship, and kind considerations over the years.

Thanks also to our charming and seemingly tireless editor, Elizabeth Spainhour of Addison Wesley Longman, who—appropriately enough—we met over the Internet and who has been a strong supporter of *Managing Knowledge* in every way, from day one.

Ultimately, of course, without loving support from all our family members, this effort would not have been possible: Susan, Madeline, Mitchel, Lee, and Cal Globe; Michelle, Sam, and Jordan Applehans; and Pam Moore.

—*Denver, Parker, and Steamboat Springs, Colorado, 1998*

The Information Age . . . . is dead and gone, replaced by the information economy . . . . The Information Age was about the building of databases. It was about the rise of computing. Today, the databases are already built; the ninth generation of personal computers is already passing through the marketplace; computing has merged with communications to create connectivity . . . . [We have] passed into the information economy. In the information economy, intellectual capital, not physical assets, drives everything.

—Jim Taylor and Watts Wacker with Howard Means,
The 500 Year Delta:
What Happens after What Comes Next

Retooling for the Information Economy

Definition

InfoSmog (in fō smôg) :
The condition of
having too much
information to be able
to take an effective
action or make an
informed decision.

Data-Induced Paralysis

The information age is now the *information economy*. The ongoing pursuit of information technology (IT) is showing no signs of slowing down. Businesses are now envisioning new ways of using it. Concepts and ideas such as supply chain management, electronic commerce, virtual corporations, and many others mark a significant new phase in the adoption of IT. This new phase involves combining the transactional and communication capabilities of IT into a new commercial infrastructure on top of which new business models can be built.

At the heart of the new phase are two dependent but conflicting trends:

- **Ongoing Proliferation of Data and Information—in terms of both content and technologies, which will not slow down but will speed up**
- **Need for Knowledge—in terms of the need to distill information and to take actions with predictable outcomes**

This new economy thrives on producing information and passing it at unprecedented rates among partners, employees, and customers. But as the volume increases, the need to identify the important pieces that allow us to act effectively in the interests of our organizations becomes more urgent.

We call this condition of the information economy "InfoSmog"—in other words, data-induced paralysis. KM has emerged as a hopeful cure. However, to date it has provided merely a set of concepts to help us diagnose the ailments. It has remained a mostly academic discussion at a very high and theoretical level. The books are typically thick and text-intensive. *Managing Knowledge* is different in that we want to be the first to offer a "getting started" approach to this topic.

The concepts, techniques, and technologies offered here derive from our experience in building an enterprise-wide *knowledge architecture* for J.D. Edwards, an enterprise resource planning software provider based in Denver, Colorado. We were not hired as consultants to come in and build this architecture from the ground up. Rather, we began as three employees in the marketing communications arm of the business who understood the long-range plans of the company and how Web-based technologies and KM principles could help J.D. Edwards achieve its goals.

You'll find in these pages a frank discussion of what we learned about getting started. Accordingly, we're not offering a total view of KM. Those looking for a summarization of all the work in this field will not find it here. Those looking for a way to understand effective leveraging of Web-based technologies as Intranets and Extranets will, we hope, be thoroughly satisfied. Those who have a general (or even vague) inkling that KM and Intranets/Extranets are complementary concepts should find this a very useful volume. Above all, those who are trying to start KM and/or Intranet/Extranet efforts will find what they need in these pages.

Why You Need *Managing Knowledge*

The *information maelstrom* began in 1964. At that point, the IBM 360/370 mainframe finally displaced competing offerings from Honeywell, Digital, Burroughs, and others. Since the advent of the 360/370, businesses have been using information technology to "retool" themselves and have developed an appetite for information technologies that appears to be far from satisfied. Early on, the efficiencies had to do with automating high-volume, relatively static processes such as airline reservations systems, claims processing, and the like.

Today, information technology has enabled businesses to re-engineer the very ways they do business. The emergence of "electronic commerce" and "supply chain management" represents the grandest vision yet of how information technology can lead to compelling new business models. Through the convergence of high-bandwidth data transmission technologies, ever-increasing processing power, and de facto interoperability standards, a new and genuine economic "infrastructure" has developed to make all of this imaginable.

This infrastructure has made it possible for us to re-envision how commerce gets done. But it has also changed the environment in which we operate and, accordingly, introduced new competitive imperatives. For our purposes, three imperatives are paramount:

- **Ease of Partnering:** Core competencies often are easier to buy than to develop in-house. To take advantage of these "external" capacities, your business must simplify the way it partners with suppliers, intermediaries, customers, and other outsourcing companies.
- **Managing Expertise Turnover:** Expertise gravitates toward the highest bidder. Businesses are paying dearly for the downsizing craze, because loyalty has been nearly completely eroded as a stabilizing force in the company. How will you replace expertise when it leaves? How will you get new hires up to speed quickly?
- **Decentralizing Decision-Making:** Reacting quickly to new opportunities demands that your company unleash decision-making authority (and competence to do so) at the front lines. How can you trust that the right decisions will be made at this level?

Taken together, these three reasons are at the heart of the KM trend taking hold of mind share over the last two years. Each of these competitive imperatives demands that enterprises provide the right content to the right people at the right time. Getting partners up to speed on your products, processes, and requirements—as well as you getting up to speed on theirs—necessitates more than simply passing highly structured purchase orders through an electronic data interchange

Today, information technology has enabled businesses to re-engineer the very ways they do business.

(EDI) system. Educating new employees and retaining the expertise of those who leave is becoming more than the function of corporate training departments. You must make sure that front-line decision-makers have the knowledge they need to act in the best interests of your company.

A Tactical Definition of Knowledge

You can't address these imperatives with technology alone. By itself, technology is only the enabling layer. *Knowledge* is the heart of the matter, and it is not nearly as easy to capture as data and information. But what do we mean by "knowledge"? For what follows in this book, we offer a tactical definition:

Knowledge is the ability to turn information and data into effective action.

We call this a "tactical definition" because we're not interested in esoteric academic debates about the nature of "epistemology." Rather, our interest is in helping you figure out how to turn information into the basis for action— actions that have desirable outcomes for your business. For this reason, we've chosen this definition. In this sense, *"managing knowledge" means delivering the information and data people need to be effective in their jobs.*

Knowledge differs from "information" and "data" in significant respects. *Data comes in the form of measurements—* pounds per square inch (psi), millions of instructions per second (MIPS), centimeters (cm), megabytes (MB), etc.

Information is a statement of fact about these measurements. Examples include:

- **By introducing stricter emissions standards, the levels (in parts per million) of particulate matter in the atmosphere were brought into compliance with EPA standards.**
- **The new quality management initiative has reduced product defects by 45%.**

These statements tell you about the effects of a particular action or set of actions, but they don't tell you how to act in future similar situations. To become knowledge in the sense that we are using it in this book, these statements must be translated into frameworks, principles, or general guidelines that allow you to take effective actions in the future.

Translating information into knowledge is conceptually an easy step, but in practice it can be very difficult. Consider an example: Configuring a network to support a maximum number of users while minimizing their response time involves careful planning. The characteristics of the existing network must be compared against the demands of a particular application and the requirements of its users. For instance, adding Enterprise Resource Planning (ERP) applications (such as J.D. Edwards OneWorld, PeopleSoft, and SAP R/3) to an existing network can significantly impact the response times for all applications if you don't plan the network infrastructure to handle the additional traffic.

To effectively plan the network infrastructure requires more than access to data and information. Software companies generally have volumes of data indicating how their applications perform over given network configurations. They may even have stacks of "case studies" documenting how specific implementations have been configured. But the network consultant really needs a set of general principles—or "rules of thumb"—that he or she can use to plan the implementation:

- **Use high-speed connections to support transactions that tend to generate a lot of network traffic**
- **Reserve WAN connections to support lower-volume transactions**

Formulated as rules of thumb, these principles provide the consultant with a set of principles that she or he can use as the basis for decision-making in any network-planning situation. The consultant would know that a high-volume transaction such as entering sales orders is best served by a high-speed LAN connection handling the traffic between the application and the appropriate data. Less frequently used

Why Manage Knowledge?

1. **Ease of partnering**
2. **Managing expertise turnover**
3. **Decentralizing decision-making**

transactions may be able to get by with lower-speed connections. Managing knowledge for these consultants means building up a collection of these rules of thumb that can be applied to produce the effects that they want, such as lower network traffic and faster response times.

Simplicity and Knowledge

Central to our understanding of knowledge is "simplicity." That is, think of the relation among data, information, and knowledge as a pyramid where data forms the foundation, information forms the middle section, and knowledge resides at the top (Figure I.1). In terms of volume, data takes up the most space, information takes a little less, and knowledge forms the small portion at the top. But standing at that vantage point allows the most commanding view of the surrounding landscape.

Knowledge can and should be evaluated by the decisions or actions to which it leads.

— Thomas Davenport

Information-driven Cyber-pioneers versus Knowledge-driven Digerati: *"Having left the hard work of pioneering the Information Age to their data-pig cousins, [the Digerati are] the most prepared to take advantage of the information economy. Unlike the cyber-pioneers, they know what is important and what is not—they are primarily knowledge driven, not primarily information driven .... (Whichever Internet provider figures out the skilled-lazy connection to the World Wide Web wins, big.)"*

— **Jim Tayler and Watts Wacker with Howard Means,** *The 500 Year Delta: What Happens after What Comes Next*

Simplicity involves providing guidelines, concepts, and principles for assimilating new data and information as knowledge—the basis for action. For instance, there are many ways to understand the stock market. But one of the most reliable has been the relation among interest rates, inflation, and corporate earnings. If people expect that interest rates will remain low or fall further, they will (other things being equal) expect corporate earnings to increase and have a tendency to invest and drive up stock values. At the same time, they begin to watch for signs of inflation. If they begin to expect that inflation will drive up rates and reduce earnings, they may get out and drive down stock valuations. Listening closely to the words of the chairman of the Federal Reserve Board becomes one way of assimilating the huge volumes of data available on the economy and preparing to take action on them.

The importance of thinking about knowledge in terms of simplicity is that you can:

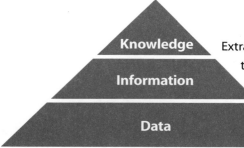 Extracting knowledge involves interpreting the volumes of data and information to arrive at concepts and guidelines that can be documented, packaged, and delivered to employees, partners, customers, and suppliers who need them. Extracting these concepts and guidelines from data and information allows you to simplify how you disseminate expertise throughout your extended supply chain.

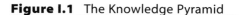

Figure I.1 The Knowledge Pyramid

- Apply concepts to similar, recurring situations to produce predictable effects.
- Apply concepts to new situations to produce innovation.
- Refine guidelines through repeated application and verification.

Although we offer a conceptually simple definition, the complexity of knowledge has to do with where it lives. The majority of it is "tacit"—residing in people's heads in the form of instinct and values. Together, instinct and values add up to experience, which is notoriously difficult to capture. Tacit knowledge is passed on mostly through informal and formal conversation.

Knowledge also lives in documents, databases, processes, and corporate culture, but it is rarely elucidated. It is often buried on page 18 of a 250-page report, or it is often unspoken instinct based on experience, or, in the case of databases, it is incapable of being extracted because of proprietary formats. Finding and translating experience, instinct, and values into "documentable" knowledge that can be delivered throughout your supply chain are at the core of managing knowledge.

People, Content, and Technology

In terms of KM, these concepts and guidelines can be easily "packaged" and distributed to existing and new employ-

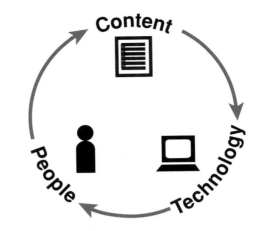

Figure I.2 Key Components of Knowledge Management

ees, customers, and partners, thus allowing them to be effective immediately. Extracting knowledge, however, is not a technological proposition—it is an interpretive and, therefore, human capacity. For this reason, we blend the following "components" (Figure I.2):

- **People: Those who produce and those who use knowledge that will be the basis for action**
- **Content: The flow of data, information, and knowledge important to the success of the business**
- **Technology: The technical infrastructure that enables the capture, storage, and delivery of content to those who need it when they need it**

We cannot overemphasize the point that technology is an enabler—not the solution. *Managing Knowledge* will discuss technology in enough detail to help you decide what pieces you'll need. But if you don't have a strong understanding of

what content you need to focus on and a core group of individuals whose main job is to turn information into knowledge, your KM initiative will fail. If you use the concepts and follow the procedures in this book, you'll know exactly where to begin and how to get started.

Navigating the Information Maelstrom

Before we begin, we'd like to share with you a story of ours that gives us a context for understanding our efforts. It derives from one of the authors' discussions with Marshall McLuhan, professor of English literature at the University of Toronto in the 1960s and 1970s, and coiner of "the global village." He was fond of Edgar Allen Poe's "A Descent into the Maelstrom." In this short story, a sailor finds his ship drawn into a vast and deadly ocean whirlpool. As powerful currents sweep him down the wall of water toward certain death on the rocks below, he observes bits of debris floating up to the surface while the heavier debris—

including his boat—circles downward. Taking note of these patterns, he acts to save himself:

It was not a new terror that thus affected me, but the dawn of a more exciting hope . . . I no longer hesitated what to do. I resolved to lash myself securely to the water cask upon which I now held, to cut it loose from the counter, and to throw myself with it into the water.

McLuhan saw in this passage an allegory for the new economy emerging at the time. For him, the sailor demonstrates the skills necessary for an era in which information is abundant, although knowledge is scarce but essential to survival. As the sheer volume of water has accumulated around him, the sailor's ability to move forward on his previous course is no longer possible. The solution, however, is not to go down with the ship, but to figure out how to operate in the new environment. Knowing what information counts— the small bits of debris floating to the surface—is the key to effective action—leaping into the maelstrom and latching oneself "securely to the water cask."

> *We are drowning in information, and starving for knowledge.*
>
> — **John Naisbitt**,
> ***Megatrends***

Just as unprecedented economic growth was accompanied by staggering amounts of pollution in the industrial age, the information age has given us InfoSmog.

We need to find the patterns and principles in the new knowledge environment that can help us survive and prosper in an information maelstrom. It is no longer good enough to give employees powerful information technologies (such as intranets, e-mail, data warehouses, and executive information systems) and expect the rest to take its natural course. Rather, what you end up giving them is Poe's maelstrom—what we call InfoSmog. Employees are left to their own devices to read the patterns in the maelstrom, or (and we bet this is more often the case)

they just don't get out of the boat.

After reading *Managing Knowledge*, you should be able to start applying basic KM concepts to organize people, content, and technologies into a targeted solution. The function of a *knowledge manager*—and the guiding principle of this book—is to understand these patterns and to help your company focus on the water cask. You'll learn how to identify the particular people and knowledge that will help your company ascend the walls of the information maelstrom. ◎

How This Book Is Organized

This book is organized into four parts, and is based on our own experiences and findings as we put together a successful Web-based KM project at J.D. Edwards:

Getting Started

Part One deals with the concepts and tools that we'll be using in this book: the *audit*, the *content portfolio*, and the *knowledge architecture*. It includes a discussion of a basic KM skill—profiling people—as well as a discussion of return on investment (ROI) for KM projects.

Organizing Around Knowledge

Part Two looks at these skills in action and shows you how to envision your company, not as an organizational hierarchy, but as a collec-

tion of cooperative "content centers." You'll learn how to "organize around knowledge" by combining content and people into the basis for your knowledge architecture.

Knowledge Architecture

In Part Three, we show you how to "bring it all together" into a unified knowledge architecture. We'll discuss translation of content centers into a networked organization, including navigation strategies and other issues surrounding the deployment of people, content, and technology.

The Ninety-Day Action Plan

Finally, in Part Four, we provide a quick checklist to help ensure a successful KM initiative.

Part One

Getting Started

The economic environment in which we live is changing drastically. The convergence of computing power, telecommunications, and interoperability standards (most compellingly in the U.S., but spreading globally) is giving businesses the power to reformulate how commerce gets done. Competing in this new environment will depend in part not simply on managing *information*, but on managing *knowledge*. You will have to turn an interpretive eye toward your information to extract the basic principles and ideas that allow employees, partners, and customers to take effective action. The first part of this book is devoted to helping you understand the scope of the effort involved.

Just as fat has replaced starvation as this nation's number one dietary concern, information overload has replaced information scarcity as an important new emotional, social, and political problem.

—David Shenk,
Data Smog:
Surviving the Information Glut

Chapter One

Strategy

Beyond Accessibility—From Information Systems to Managing Knowledge

As traditionally defined, the CIO is in charge of the technology your company uses to capture, store, and access data. His or her job usually involves developing standards—maybe you've standardized on Unix servers with Oracle databases. It also involves controlling costs—delivering the best solution for the smallest amount of money. Above all, his or her job is to help the company assimilate information technology (IT) to cut costs, achieve competitive advantage, or change the business model.

The effect of this assimilation has been a general increase in the *volume* and *accessibility* of information. This is inevitable in the sense that it is a natural effect of the information economy—the production of more and more infor-mation to support employees, partners, and customers. On the other side of this equation, it has given us InfoSmog—data-induced paralysis. There is simply too much information to take quick and effective actions in the interests of our organizations.

As the assimilation of IT continues, the need to extract the kind of infor-mation that allows people to take actions that lead to predictable out-comes is becoming paramount. We don't need to reduce the amount of information and data we collect. We need to learn how to translate data and information into knowledge—those general principles that, when applied, yield predictable results.

As we've already said, this is *not* pri-marily a technology issue, although it involves technology. It is a human capac-ity that must be judiciously applied. For example, plenty of information exists on

The need to extract the kind of information that allows people to take actions is becoming paramount.

the effectiveness of airbags. We can state increased survival rates for adults as facts, and we can collect the data in databases. But knowledge comes in the form of a general principle: young children stand a better chance of surviving accidents if they are placed in the back seat with a seat belt fastened. It's a fairly simple principle that is derived from experience and lab tests. When applied, the outcome should be predictable—an increased rate of survival. Because it is stated simply, it can be packaged and disseminated easily by means of public service announcements, casual conversation, videos, etc.

Managing knowledge—as we define it in this book—in the context of business involves capturing and disseminating these principles (along with related data and information) based on job functions. That is, you need to define those job functions that are essential to the realization of your organization's goals and objectives, and you must figure out the knowledge they need to be successful. While this involves making information and data accessible, it more importantly involves distilling it for them into knowledge.

The Audit—Matching KM Projects to Business Objectives

It is easy to think too big about KM and therefore to start too big. Remember, managing knowledge is about getting the right information to the right people so they can do their jobs effectively. As described in the existing literature, KM can easily become intimidating because it's too overwhelming. The purpose of the audit is to help you break KM down into digestible, manageable projects without losing sight of the "big picture." It is designed to help you focus quickly on what counts and to adjust your vision as business conditions change. There are four basic questions regarding the audit:

- **What are the success factors of your organization (company, division, and/or department) and the relevant business cycles?**
- **What are the important points in these cycles where actions must be swift and effective?**
- **Who will use the content?**
- **What is the important content used at these points?**

There is simply too much information to take quick and effective actions.

These questions may seem surprisingly obvious, but few companies understand them as key to valuing their "intellectual capital." Answering these questions means supplementing information technology skills with other competencies. The first two questions focus on *context:* what are the most important recurring events, situations, and circumstances in which knowledge is produced and consumed in your company, and how are they related to your organization's goals and objectives? The third question addresses the *people:* who are the important people in these critical contexts? The fourth question addresses *content:* what information is critical to the success of these people in these contexts?

The first question can be one of the most difficult to answer. Nevertheless, we can't overemphasize this point: don't go any further with KM until you can answer this question. Until you can do so with confidence, your KM initiatives will at worst flounder and fail, and at best will end up as a series of half-baked, poorly coordinated projects. Always remember that the audit is the linchpin between your company's/division's/department's objectives and your KM projects. Example business objectives that will help you to start identifying KM projects are as follows:

- **We will be the easiest automotive parts supplier with whom the big three can build lasting partnerships.**
- **We will be recognized as the most responsive package delivery service in the world.**

- **We will provide a higher standard of care than any other physician group in our market.**

Such a statement can provide the starting point for determining which business cycles will be important and what information will be important to capture. Identifying these cycles allows you to identify what Thomas H. Davenport has called "information leverage points" (ILPs)—"information that, once identified, provides a superior map of the roads to business success" (*CIO Magazine*, June 1, 1996). We've adapted this term to help you identify those points in your important business cycles where data, information, and knowledge must be delivered for your business objectives to be met.

For instance, in highly competitive industries, sales cycles tend to be very resource-intensive. Companies in this situation need to learn how to assess their chances of winning deals early. In other words, "qualifying prospects" is an important ILP. Before getting involved, the sales team needs to know a lot of things. One of the most important is which competitors are involved, and what success rates you've had against them in similar situations. This includes more than just statistical data. It requires assessments of the context of wins and losses against those competitors. These "win/loss interviews" can provide the knowledge that allows the sales team to qualify the opportunity: "Pursue the opportunity if it's a construction firm

Information Leverage Points (ILPs)—"information that, once identified, provides a superior map of the roads to business success."

—Thomas H. Davenport , *CIO Magazine,* June 1, 1996

Do not start until you understand the objectives of your company, department, or work group.

Only when you understand the business objectives of your company, division, or department can you begin to identify and scope KM projects. Do not start until you can do this with confidence.

If you are unsure of how to find this information, there are a few places to begin looking. You can find your company's business objectives in the form of vision statements, annual reports, executive interviews with the trade press, long-range plan (LRP) statements, strengths—weaknesses—opportunities—threats (SWOTS) statements, and other documents in which future direction and market position are discussed.

with a high degree of international operations—we are stronger than our competitors here." "Don't try to sell to companies with more than 1000 employees or $200 million in annual revenue—our manufacturing capacity generally can't support their volume requirements." Delivering this kind of information and knowledge in reference to an important ILP can improve the performance of the business.

The Content Portfolio— Knowing What's Important

The content portfolio is the combination of data, information, and knowledge you are seeking to manage. It represents the specific pieces and types of content that your company must effectively package and deliver to people who can act on them as knowledge. This can include regulatory documents, release schedules, competitive intelligence, technical product specifications, software applications, case studies, etc.

The content portfolio is not about indexing everything. It is not about applying Web-based search engines to all of your documents and databases. Others have tried this as KM quick fixes. It doesn't work. The content portfolio is a formal recognition that knowledge, information, and data have relative value—relative, that is, in terms of your company's goals and objectives.

An example: If executive management has decided that your photocopier company will succeed on the basis of minimizing customer downtime for maintenance and repair, then knowing and sharing troubleshooting skills will be more important than knowledge of emerging photocopier markets or new product development. You're more likely to focus on improving existing products. Accordingly, your KM strategy should understand the cycle of how troubleshooting information is produced and circulated currently—particularly the barriers preventing its flow to field support personnel and back to product development. You'll want to figure out how to document any fixes found in the field and get them back to customer service and product development for verification and circulation back out to the field. You may even begin considering customer "self-service" strategies that would make this troubleshooting information available to customers. ILPs will include, for example, the moment someone figures out the cause of a recurring problem, and the moment someone figures out how to solve it. Moving such knowledge can be the key to achieving your business objectives.

The Knowledge Architecture—The Scope of the Effort

Success in the emerging information economy is based on effective packaging and delivery of content to the critical users who must use it. You should not try

The content portfolio is a formal recognition that knowledge, information, and data have relative value.

CONTENT portfolio

You'll know that managing knowledge is producing a positive ROI when you see:

①
Measurable efficiencies in product development, production, sales, and service cycles.

②
Improved decision-making at the front lines in your development, production, sales, and support cycles.

③
Better ability to get new partners up to speed quickly.

④
Improved morale because employees are making more effective decisions.

⑤
Increasing customer loyalty due to better trust in your employees' expertise.

to do this casually. You need to formalize your effort and give it a name. We call it the "knowledge architecture": *The knowledge architecture represents your company's formal recognition that it has important experience and expertise that it must preserve and use to its advantage.*

As such, the knowledge architecture identifies the scope of the investment that will be made in managing knowledge. This is more than a technical solution. It involves three components:

- **People**
- **Content**
- **Technology**

Managing knowledge means blending each of the components into a cohesive unit whose main purpose is to understand the important content necessary to meet objectives, the key people who are the suppliers and users of the content, and the technologies appropriate to meet the KM objectives.

Everything that follows in this book is designed to help you diagram your knowledge architecture and to begin understanding what the initial time and investment will be. We will provide techniques for building 1) road maps to finding important content, 2) job descriptions for people who will supply the content to your organization, and 3) practical evaluations of the relevant technologies for KM. Remember throughout that the technology of KM is only as good as the people who use and manage the content that rides on top of it. Above all, building a successful knowledge architecture means assessing the important content for the success of your organization, then putting people and technology behind that information.

Return on Investment

The inevitable question arises: What is this going to cost and is it worth the investment? This is usually followed up with another question: How can I measure my results to determine if the strategy has been effective? In our experience at J.D. Edwards, these can be very difficult questions to answer. As far as measuring the return on an Intranet/Extranet, we have measured the cost savings in terms of employee time saved (7 to 10 hours a month multiplied by the appropriate salaries) as well as printing costs saved ($900,000 in the first year). According to International Data Corporation, who performed our first-year ROI measurements, these cost savings alone yielded an ROI of over 1800%—including content and technical professionals, firewall technologies, management, hardware, software, and other expenses.

That return alone justified the cost of our Intranet/Extranet—technology and people included. But how do you measure the return on "managing knowledge"? This is much more difficult because the benefits are much less classically measurable. They are, as we outlined them in the Introduction:

- **Faster, simplified partnering strategies**
- **Greater retention of expertise**
- **Better and more effective frontline decision-making**

It certainly seems possible to measure these benefits, but why would you want to? It's enough to know that these areas are being improved.

Very few, if any, trusted measurements exist for determining ROI on IT investments. In fact, most companies have been investing in IT (people included) and absorbing it at a rate unprecedented for anything else in history. But this is occurring in *inverse proportion* to our ability to measure ROI. For example, the ROI for the adoption of the first mainframes and minicomputers was pretty straightforward: you could process more transactions per day with fewer people. But what's the ROI on an e-mail system? Businesses are adopting Lotus Notes and Microsoft Exchange much faster than they ever adopted mainframes, and no one seems to be sweating the measurements. At best, they can measure fairly conventional statistics such as inventory turnover, transactions per day, and customer base, but these are industrial economy considerations. In the information economy, as we understand it, you need to measure speed of knowledge transfer in such areas as new employee hires, new business partners, and customer satisfaction. ◎

Building a successful knowledge architecture means assessing important content, then putting people and technology behind that information.

Business Objective: Reduce airline turnaround time

To remain profitable, airlines must keep their planes in the air as much of the time as possible. After all, a jumbo jet is not a cheap asset, and it pays off only when it is filled with paying passengers. Therefore, turnaround time on the ground—at the gate or in the hanger for maintenance—is an important ILP for airlines. That is, the faster a mechanic can finish a repair, the faster the plane can get going. Making the mechanic hunt through volumes of documentation for the one paragraph he or she may be looking for isn't helping profitability. In this case, the airline has a critical need to focus KM resources on preventing airline mechanics from "hunting and gathering." The company has a vested interest in making the needed information readily accessible to them on a just-in-time basis.

Business Objective: Capture 10% of the pharmaceutical market

Let's say that your company has pegged pharmaceutical companies as a key market. Your introductory sales demonstrations are probably important, and recurring, ILPs. For these demos, your sales reps will need to be armed with competitive intelligence and an understanding of issues facing the pharmaceutical industry. They will also need information concerning how the features of your product match the needs of prospective customers. Thus, attempting to understand the total scope of the knowledge and the information that will make these sales reps successful in their sales demonstrations to pharmaceutical prospects could be one objective of your knowledge audit.

Business Objective: Never get beaten by Globe Generators in deals over $100,000

Globe Generators is failing. Customers are dissatisfied with their inability to deliver customized generators on time and on budget. Your executive committee figures that if Globe can be eliminated early, your company stands a 50% better chance of winning these larger deals.

The first step in the audit is to determine the relevant business cycle. That's easy in this case—the sales cycle. Next you need to figure out the ILPs in that cycle where you face competition from Globe. Perhaps the most important point of competition is the product demonstration. This is where you will focus on delivering the content necessary to eliminate them from the deal. The KM goal will be to capture and distribute to sales reps the "silver bullets" that will expose Globe's weaknesses while highlighting your own strengths.

What does KM look like, given these business objectives? It looks like a good competitive intelligence group. It should involve a team of people dedicated to devising the general principles that, when applied, will expose the weaknesses of the competitor and frequently lead to their elimination from further consideration. This team will collect all forms of bad press on Globe (largely via the World Wide Web), store it in a database, and push summaries out to sales reps on a regular basis. They will perform win/loss interviews and write up feature/function comparisons between your products and Globe's. As "knowledge analysts" (a position we'll discuss later), they are driving toward the extraction of those general principles, or silver bullets, that sales reps can use over and over again to win against Globe.

I tell people about the intelligent pager that I have and love: how it delivers in full sentences of perfect English only timely and relevant information . . . . The way it works is that only one human being has its number and all messages go through that person, who knows where I am [and] what is important [to me].

—Nicholas Negroponte,
Being Digital

Chapter Two

Profiling People

Profiling is the key to executing a successful audit. Effective profiling of key partners, employees, and customers will give you a clear picture of which KM projects are the right starting points. To begin to understand this skill, consider yourself. Think about the information and documents that you try to have near you over the course of your day. What's in your briefcase? What databases do you access? On what applications do you rely? What have you "bookmarked" in your browser? Whom do you call for answers? With whom do you collaborate? What magazines do you read? What e-mail newsletters do you receive? Each of these items makes up your professional content interests—data, information, and knowledge repositories that you regularly use to be successful and stay "informed."

The next set of questions is tougher. Why do you use each of these items? What role does each one play? What are their strengths and weaknesses? Which ones are essential to your success? Which ones are merely helpful? Profiling—as we're using the term for the audit—means asking and answering these kinds of questions for your important users. Like the portfolio of information you rely on daily, the enterprise version comprises the list of specific content that your company will strive to manage on behalf of those who are responsible for meeting business goals and objectives.

Whom Do You Profile?

Finding out whom to profile can be trickier than you think. It's not simply a matter of picking up the HR handbook of job descriptions. More often than not, these descriptions may be pale approximations of how people are actually working. Instead, you must begin by understanding the specific business objectives that your company or department or division is "on the hook" for accomplishing. For instance, a chemical manufacturer may have a long range plan (LRP) that includes reducing its Environmental Protection Agency violations by 50% over the next three years. Your questions should focus on the people responsible for making this happen and what information and knowledge they'll need to make it happen. Without understanding goals and objectives, you will have a very difficult time identifying the proper people to profile.

How Do You Profile?

Profiling can be accomplished in many different ways. The most effective profiling looks like "a day in the life." What are employees' sources of frustration?

Where do processes seem to go very smoothly? What meetings do people never miss? What meetings do they generally ignore? Finding this information may involve traveling to remote plants and offices to observe people's daily lives. It can involve finding existing knowledge exchanges and tapping into them. These exchanges can include e-mail distribution lists, conference calls, and regular meetings between or among particular job functions (product developers, marketing consultants, customer service representatives).

One way to *fail* at profiling is to send out an e-mail survey and expect people to answer it in a way that helps you. It's not that they will be dishonest—they just won't give you the information you need. Market researchers have known this for a

One way to *fail* at profiling is to send out an e-mail survey and expect people to answer it in a way that helps you. It's not that they will be dishonest—they just won't give you the information you need.

SAMPLE QUESTIONS

What documents do you carry with you in your briefcase on a regular basis?

What documents do you keep on your hard drive? Which ones do you make absolutely sure to back up?

Of all the information available to you, what are the most important documents you try to have with you at all times? Why are they most important? How do you keep track of them?

What are three or four typical situations in which lack of information hurts you with prospects/customers or hinders your ability to do your job effectively?

If you need to call someone for information, how do you know whom to call? What do you do if you don't know?

How do you typically learn about new functionalities or enhancements to our products? How would you prefer to learn about new functionalities or enhancements?

How do you learn about our competitors? What are typical issues you try to learn about them?

What are the three or four most important items of information that Customer Service can provide to you? How about Training? Marketing?

If a prospect were to ask about our products, what information would you want to provide for them? To whom would you go for such information, or where would you expect to find it?

Is there information that is not in our Intranet (Extranet) that you regularly use? What is it?

What noncorporate information do you regularly use (SIC codes, databases, industry reports, etc.)?

How frequently do you use a browser to find information, internally or externally? Do you regularly use "Favorites"? What sites have proven valuable to you?

Sample Employee Profile:
Sales Rep

Sales personnel have a strong need for four general types of information: 1) positioning, 2) product and service partners, 3) production schedules, and 4) market intelligence. This group is responsible for taking a prospect from a qualified lead to a closed sale. Their information needs revolve around positioning products against competitors. Additionally, engaging partners, discussing product availability and schedules, and learning from others' sales experiences (successful and unsuccessful) are critical.

To help these people be successful, our company should manage the following kinds of information for them:

- **Customer references**
- **Industry issues, statutory guidelines, and case studies**
- **Market analyses, including articles, competitive feature comparisons, and contacts**
- **Partners, including contacts, benefits, references, and case studies**
- **Functionality and production schedules**

A complete profile should discuss each of these bulleted points in detail.

long time. For instance, if you ask a random group of 1000 car owners what they'd like to see in a new car, the vast majority will tell you of the enhancements they want—a bigger trunk, better gas mileage, more room in the back seat. What you won't be offered is the kind of information that would allow you to start thinking about genuine competitive advantage—never going to a gas station again, never buying tires, an exhaust-free automobile.

If you stick to profiling long-time employees, you may miss the "outsider" perspective that new employees, partners, and customers can bring to the table.

A better way to search for insight is to do focused interviews with a small group of partners, customers, and/or employees within each important job function. These are the people who can give you suggestions that lead to a successful audit. They can tell you what the typical "day in the life" looks like for others in their position. These are the people who are already doing their jobs as best they can. They've maxed out the productivity potentials of their jobs given the existing knowledge architecture—or lack thereof. To find these people, ask around. You'll generally find a consensus as to who are the brightest and most articulate people in any job category.

Don't simply segregate interviews, surveys, and observations by job function. You need to put dependent job functions in dialog with each other. Otherwise you'll end up understanding what a customer support rep needs, but you won't benefit from the innovation that may come out of combining different people who do different but related tasks. Also, don't limit your interviews to veterans or long-time business partners and customers. Some of the most valuable contributors come from those who are new to your company and are trying to get up to speed on your products but are unclear of how best to do so. These people may have worked for your competitors and can help you benchmark the quality of your information- and knowledge-sharing practices against others in your industry. Further, if you stick to profiling long-time employees, you may miss the "outsider" perspective that new employees, partners, and customers can bring to the table.

Learn how your colleagues successfully sell, develop, or support your product or service. Look to human resources, business operations, and key managers to help identify and profile the expectations/quotas of these drivers. This may sound easy, but our experience says that you need to be diligent. It's hard work. In this chapter we provide some of the questions you'll want to ask. ◎

Additional Information Needs

Consider the information and knowledge needs of those outside your company, including:

Customers

Investors

Regulatory agencies

Other government agencies

Suppliers

Business partners

Resellers

Industry and financial analysts

Trade press

Recruits

Competitors

Sources for profiles might include:

Informally Talk to People: Management, key decision-makers, top sales reps, consulting managers, business partners, and customers—whomever you've determined to be the key people in accomplishing your business objectives.

Consult Human Resources: They may have job requirements on file that can help you start building reliable user profiles.

Training Departments: They often have "training paths" or certification programs for different kinds of employees, customers, and partners. They may have done research on job positions that you can leverage for your own purposes.

Focus Groups: This classic marketing tool can help you find out what a successful "day in the life" looks like to those who are responsible for accomplishing your company's or division's goals.

Part Two

Organizing Around Knowledge

Most people think of KM as a technology problem. But it begins with people and content before you start setting up the technical infrastructure. Part Two focuses on putting together two diagrams that will help you determine important people and content in relation to business cycles and objectives:

- **Knowledge Storyboard**—Shows you where content is used in your business processes and cycles
- **Knowledge Network**—Shows you where content lives in your organization and who owns it

With these diagrams in hand, you'll be able to identify where you are currently doing well in managing your company's knowledge; you'll also be able to understand where you need improvement. These items sharpen your understanding and are your guides to getting the right information to the right people at the right time.

Using the diagrams, you won't spend time working on a knowledge architecture that delivers unnecessary information—such as the mailroom's vision statement, pictures of someone's trip to New Zealand, and other things that tend to show up on corporate Intranets. The knowledge audit is the methodology for defining how KM projects will map to business processes. In the next few chapters, we'll step you through the process of the audit.

Knowledge assets, like money or equipment, exist and are worth cultivating only in the context of strategy.

—Thomas A. Stewart,
*Intellectual Capital:
The New Wealth of Organizations*

Chapter Three

Storyboarding Knowledge

How many of us know what will be the key revenue drivers for our companies over the next few months? Understanding your LRP, revenue drivers, cost-cutting areas, market conditions, and business objectives is essential to a successful project—you can't get started without this knowledge. With an understanding of specific business objectives, you can begin to evaluate your important ILPs. Remember, getting the right information to the right people at the right time is the objective. This chapter will show you how to link your KM projects to identifiable business objectives.

Mapping People and Content

The immediate purpose of the knowledge audit is to identify the knowledge, information, and data that will add the greatest value to your organization's bottom line.

The result will be, in most cases, a "storyboard." The emphasis will be on the intellectual capital, its users, and consumers. Your storyboard will diagram the relationships among people, processes, and knowledge. Accordingly, it will consist of four steps:

Step One: Pick a business cycle or process and understand how it works.

Step Two: Break the cycle down to every event where people need to act.

Step Three: Identify the people who use information at each point.

Step Four: Select the content necessary to act at each ILP.

The storyboard puts these four elements in relation to each other, thus showing *who* needs *what* information and *when* they need it. You can use this as a blueprint for implementing a knowledge architecture.

Getting the right information to the right people at the right time is the objective.

Identifying Your Strategic Business Cycles

Pick a business cycle or process

and understand how it works.

Why Is This Important?

Understanding the objectives of your organization (enterprise, department, division, workgroup) allows you to focus on small KM projects without losing sight of the big picture. Based on your organization's specific goals, review one key business cycle and process on which you'll focus. You may focus on a sales cycle, a manufacturing cycle, or a distribution cycle for a single product. You may choose a research and development (R&D) cycle, a quality cycle, an employee lifecycle, or some other cycle.

These cycles may not be formalized or explained anywhere; the one you pick may be outside your area of expertise, and you probably won't be able to outline it just by sitting at your desk. Set up small meetings with your in-house experts, executives, or others who can steer you in the right direction if you need help understanding how your orga-

nization works in this area. Lay out the cycle on a whiteboard. If your LRP stresses quality and your customers have a low tolerance for defects, you'll need to focus on the quality management cycle. If your company's revenue over the next few years will be driven less by new sales and more by selling to your existing customer base, you'll need to look at what your customers value. You may even need to evaluate your suppliers' cycles.

Steps to Get You There

1. Examine your LRP and other specific business objectives.
2. Identify at a high level the cycles that support those objectives.
3. Pick a single cycle on which you will begin to focus (Figure 3.1).

Figure 3.1 Sample Enterprise Software Sales Cycle

- Get outside of your area of expertise—your company may drive revenue through a cycle you don't fully understand. You'll need to collaborate with people outside your department, workgroup, and company.
- Follow the money—what products and services are most profitable? How can you build a KM initiative to make these products and services even more profitable?
- What is the importance of people and organizations outside of your enterprise, department, or division? Understand what roles they play in achieving business objectives.
- What competitors will you need to confront to achieve your goals? Understanding how to leverage information to defeat them can be a key objective.

Within the one business cycle you pick to begin your KM project, identify the ILPs. If your customers thrive on quick delivery, your knowledge audit will need to focus on the ILPs in your delivery cycle. In this case:

- **Map out the ILPs; what does the delivery cycle look like? (Ask one person in your company.)**
- **Add the knowledge workers; what personnel are involved in your delivery cycle? (Ask around.) What are their job descriptions and responsibilities? (Ask HR, or pull from your Intranet.)**
- **Identify the "content portfolio." What information affects the cycle, and at what point in the cycle? (Ask a couple of different people, at least to make a start. See diagram for how to lay out.)**
- **Are there documents and expertise regarding the cycle, or various points in the cycle, that are currently scattered around the company? (Easy answer: YES!)**
- **Would people save time if this information could be collected at one easy-to-access place, instead of making them hunt all over for it? (Easy answer: YES!)**
- **How can the needed information be delivered—Web page, e-mail, Personal Data Assistant, new reports, better use of existing database, leverage marketing efforts, other ways—to help those involved in the cycle do their jobs better?**

CASE IN POINT

If new, innovative products will drive revenue for your company, you may need to focus on the R&D cycle. How will your company conduct its research? How will you gather intellectual capital to support research? How will you translate research-based knowledge into product development plans? How will you compress learning cycles and how will you improve productivity? How will you share R&D information with other divisions that can benefit from it? Answering these questions will help you define the specific areas in which to build successful projects.

Mapping Your Information Leverage Points

Purpose:

Break the cycle down to every event

where people need to act.

Why Is This Important?

This step helps you build a framework for understanding how information is used in your chosen business process. Start by identifying those events where people need to act effectively to move the process along. You're driving toward an understanding of how content fits into each part of that business cycle and how to prioritize it (Figure 3.2). Only when you understand when and where people need to act can you understand the information they need.

Things to Consider

- Don't get hung up on perfection. Most business processes aren't precise.
- Focus on a consensus or a general understanding.
- Ask yourself and others where information is acted on in your chosen business cycle.

Steps to Get You There

1. Get involved and learn how the business cycle works.
2. Interview others to find out what's important.
3. Ask about inefficiencies in the cycle. Many people have a good understanding of where they succeed or fail in such cycles.

IN POINT

Let's say you're focusing on the customer support cycle. For a highly technical product—such as software or a copy machine—this cycle contains:

Diagnosis: The customer support rep isolates the problem through a variety of techniques, including interviewing users and looking "under the covers" to find out what might be wrong. In many cases—especially with more seasoned reps—successful diagnosis may be the result of undocumented "know how" that she or he has picked up over the years.

Research: Once the problem is isolated, the rep needs to know how to fix the problem. This might involve consulting manuals, consulting a discussion database (e.g., Lotus Notes), or calling someone else.

Escalation: If the first-line customer support person can't fix the problem, he or she may escalate it to another customer support rep. This person might have access to more sophisticated databases of diagnostic and repair information, including casebases.

Figure 3.2 Mapping ILPs to the Sales Cycle

Adding the People

Purpose:

Identify the people who use information at each point.

Why Is This Important?

Once you've identified the business cycle (in Step One) and the points within it where information is most intensely used (in Step Two), you're ready to identify the people who "consume" information at each point (Figure 3.3). Who is responsible for successfully negotiating each point in the business cycle? What are the relevant job titles? Write them on the map showing how they connect to the different ILPs.

Things to Consider

- HR may be helpful here. Use existing job descriptions as clues to who's involved in the cycle.
- Training may have career paths and certification programs that are relevant.
- Talk to managers who govern the cycle. They should have a handle on who's involved and what the issues are.
- Don't narrow your focus to people in your company alone. Consider people outside the company.

IN POINT

For instance, a product demonstration is a typical ILP. For a door-to-door salesperson selling vacuum cleaners, the demonstration is pretty straightforward. There aren't too many information requirements in such a context, because this is a sell based more on "wit and charm" than on information. But take the example of a highly sophisticated product dealing with many intangibles, such as a sales force automation system. Before any company commits hundreds of thousands of dollars for licensing fees, implementation costs, and ongoing support payments, they'll want proof that the software can handle their specific requirements. To pull off a successful demonstration of this product requires a trained team including a sales representative, a software developer, an expert in the product's functionality, someone knowledgeable about the prospect's industry, installation consultants, and others. In this situation, the information requirements are intense and the players are numerous. If your knowledge project is focused on the sales cycle, you'll be wanting to organize the information that makes the sales team successful, and you'll be organizing it for "maximum consumption in minimum time." Having just laid out the ILPs for your sales cycle is what makes this possible.

Steps to Get You There

1. Interview people who govern the cycle.
2. Talk to people who are recognized performers in the cycle. What can they tell you about who is involved?
3. Add the relevant job titles to the map.

Figure 3.3 Adding People to the Enterprise Software Sales Cycle

Identifying the Content

Purpose:

Select the content necessary to act at each ILP.

Why Is This Important?

After you've identified the people involved at each point in the cycle, you'll need to identify the information they need (Figure 3.4). Spend some time figuring out the most important pieces of information used at each point in the cycle. You can do this most efficiently by talking to the people that you identified in Step Three. They are your best source for discovering what information they need to be successful. Use the techniques discussed in Chapter Two on profiling to determine this information. Write it on the map and associate it with the different ILPs in the cycle.

Things to Consider

- Profiling the people allows you to refine your entire picture of the business cycle at its ILPs.
- This map gives you a picture of what it means to get the right information to the right people at the right time.
- Focus on understanding the content that helps people act.

Steps to Get You There

1. Set up focus groups made up of the people you've identified in Step Three.
2. Devise interview questions that help you determine what information is necessary for them to act. (See Chapter Two on profiling for a sample list of these questions.)
3. Finish the storyboard by filling in the specific pieces of content needed at each ILP (Figure 3.5).

IN POINT

To continue with our sales force automation example, the demonstration team will need many different kinds of information to be successful:

- **Knowledge of the prospect's particular needs**
- **Information regarding the prospect's industry**
- **Competitive intelligence on the other players in the game**
- **Technical specifications**
- **Feature and function schedules**

This list is by no means exhaustive. The sources here can be numerous and might include product specification sheets, release schedules, contacts with other salespeople who have been in similar situations, and contacts with existing customers who would provide good references for your product.

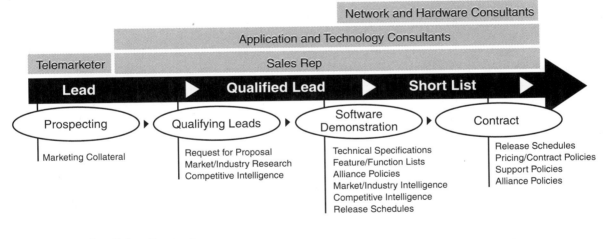

Figure 3.4 Identifying Content

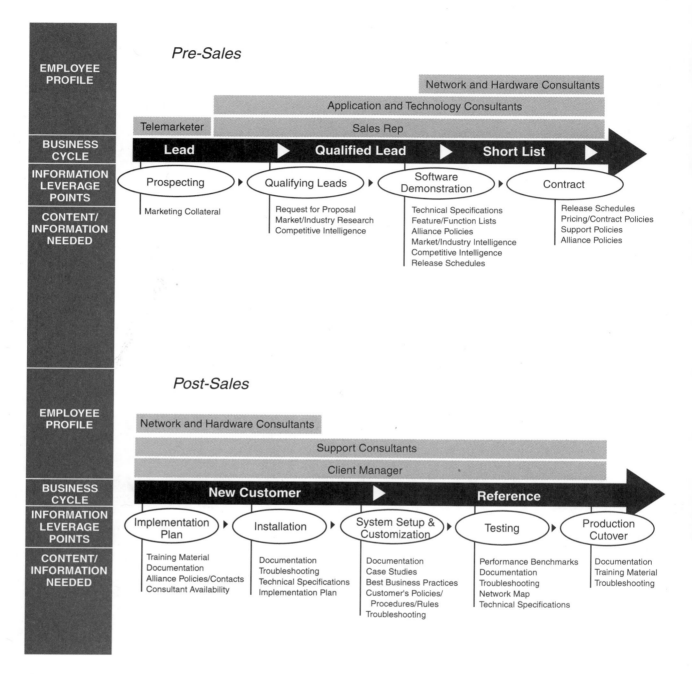

Pre-Sales

EMPLOYEE PROFILE			
			Network and Hardware Consultants
		Application and Technology Consultants	
Telemarketer	Sales Rep		

BUSINESS CYCLE			
Lead ▷	**Qualified Lead** ▷	**Short List** ▷	

INFORMATION LEVERAGE POINTS			
Prospecting ▷	Qualifying Leads ▷	Software Demonstration ▷	Contract

CONTENT/ INFORMATION NEEDED			
Marketing Collateral	Request for Proposal Market/Industry Research Competitive Intelligence	Technical Specifications Feature/Function Lists Alliance Policies Market/Industry Intelligence Competitive Intelligence Release Schedules	Release Schedules Pricing/Contract Policies Support Policies Alliance Policies

Post-Sales

EMPLOYEE PROFILE			
Network and Hardware Consultants			
Support Consultants			
Client Manager			

BUSINESS CYCLE			
New Customer ▷		**Reference**	

INFORMATION LEVERAGE POINTS				
Implementation Plan ▷	Installation ▷	System Setup & Customization ▷	Testing ▷	Production Cutover

CONTENT/ INFORMATION NEEDED				
Training Material Documentation Alliance Policies/Contacts Consultant Availability	Documentation Troubleshooting Technical Specifications Implementation Plan	Documentation Case Studies Best Business Practices Customer's Policies/ Procedures/Rules Troubleshooting	Performance Benchmarks Documentation Troubleshooting Network Map Technical Specifications	Documentation Training Material Troubleshooting

Figure 3.5 Bringing It All Together: The Knowledge Map

Knowledge is power.

—*Francis Bacon*

. . . . the information revolution favors and strengthens network forms of organization, while making life difficult for hierarchical forms . . . . It means conflicts will increasingly be waged by "networks," rather than by "hierarchies." It means that whoever masters the network form stands to gain major advantages in the new epoch.

—John Arquilla and David Ron,
In Athena's Camp: Preparing for Conflict in the Information Age

Chapter Four

Mapping the Knowledge Network

The Web transcends many boundaries. Once you begin sharing information through a browser, it becomes obvious that traditional departmental structures can hinder the efficient flow of information, data, and knowledge to the right people at the right time. Individuals no longer care about the departmental origins of content, they simply need to get to it. You shouldn't have to care that customer service owns troubleshooting information and marketing owns positioning. You simply need to get to that content—often at the same time. To deliver content effectively by means of Intranets and Extranets, you need to look at your company in terms of the information and knowledge it has. Product content typically resides in several different departments, but the browser allows you to make that information available from a single location.

The objective of mapping your knowledge network is to visualize your company's knowledge and begin assigning responsibilities to people who maintain different kinds of content. You will be able to see the complexity of the information and knowledge you're seeking to manage. This diagram will, accordingly, help you identify your staffing needs. What positions will you have to invent? Where will you need to focus resources to ensure that content gets captured and delivered? How will you distribute your KM team throughout the organization?

The steps involved in diagramming the knowledge network include:

Step One:

Identifying Content Centers: High-level centers of information, such as Product, Sales and Marketing, and Employee Resources

Step Two:

Adding Content Satellites: Lower-level centers that fall under high-level centers, such as Product Documentation, Training, and Customer Support

Step Three:

Staffing and Assigning Ownership: People who have expertise over each satellite center and are responsible for the accuracy and consistency of the information encompassed by their satellites

The challenge is to create a corporate knowledge structure that combines the best of the existing hierarchy and blends it with new, network-based forms of organization, in terms of both online information and human project teams. Creating this diagram will help transform your organization from a traditional corporate hierarchy into a powerful, flexible, and hard-hitting knowledge-sharing organization.

Staffing the Knowledge Network

If you want to maintain editorial quality of information, do not open your system up to anyone and everyone who wants to publish information to the rest of the company. This approach has appeal, but will create more InfoSmog. (This applies to employees sending global e-mails as well. If a few people are regularly clogging up e-mail with recurring, poorly crafted, global messages about benefits, events, and general info, have them send it to one person who edits and combines these missives into one daily e-mail blast for everyone.) In 1997 and 1998, some corporate Intranets had to scrap everything and start over after giving all employees access to publish their vacation photos, baby pictures, and favorite movie lists; perhaps these were good for morale, but where was the business value in such information? We suggest scaling over time to perhaps 10% of employees, most working their regular jobs while acting as part-time "knowledge authors." After training, they are the only ones who have the permission to publish information of value to the rest of the enterprise.

Identifying Content Centers

Purpose:

Build the organizational framework for capturing and delivering information.

Why Is This Important?

Once you've identified what content you need to deliver to help people act, you need to understand where it lives and how you will capture it. The first step is to pick five to eight categories that provide the basis for organizing knowledge (Figure 4.1). Some examples include:

- **Product Center**
- **Customer Center**
- **Market Intelligence Center**
- **Employee Resources Center**

Think of these categories as "centers of gravity" around which information, data, and knowledge orbit. Many departments contribute to these centers, but these categories don't always map to discrete departments. By picking these few categories, you have the basis for building the necessary processes for capturing and delivering content. Each

document or piece of data that goes into your Intranet or Extranet should fit into one of these categories. This mapping effort will serve to yield numerous benefits down the road, not the least of which is facilitation of improved searching over your information, as well as subscription and personalization.

Steps to Get You There

1. Pick five to eight categories that will be the basis for organizing around knowledge.
2. Fit your knowledge network on one sheet of paper.

IN POINT

At the most basic level, a typical manufacturing company makes products, markets them, sells them, and has employees that put all this together. Accordingly, this manufacturing firm might have seven content centers:

- **Product Center**
- **Sales and Marketing Center**
- **Employee Center**
- **R&D Center**
- **Customer Center**
- **Trading Partners Center**
- **Finance and Administration Center**

Every important piece of information, data, and content should fit into one or more of these categories. You'll need to break them down further in the next step. The important thing is to put together a basic framework for going forward.

Things to Consider

- Make the diagram of the five to eight categories fit on a single sheet of 8 1/2 x 11 inch paper. This will keep you focused on the highest levels of organizing around knowledge.
- Sticking to your categories will help you see the complexity of the information and knowledge that you're seeking to manage.
- In picking your categories, consider how your company, partners, and customers work. Are you product-centric? Customer-centric? Organized by project? By process? Addressing these questions with your knowledge workers and managers will help you arrive at a solution that places your highest-level thoughts into a framework.

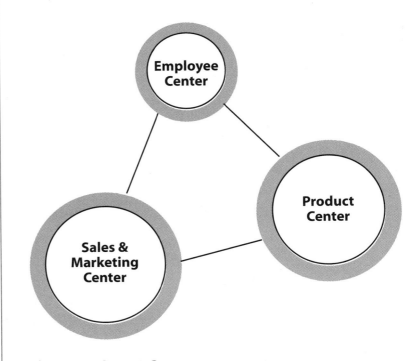

Figure 4.1 Content Centers

Adding Content Satellites

Purpose:

Break down content centers

into lower levels of detail.

Make your company look like the knowledge it produces, not the departments that produce the knowledge.

Why Is This Important?

Orbiting each center are content satellites. These satellites represent subsets of information, not necessarily departments, although they could be departments if that works well for you (Figure 4.2). In the Sales and Marketing Center, the satellites could be the topics that most help your salespeople sell—brochures, demonstration scripts, and customer reference lists. They might also include sample contracts, "Request for Proposal" boilerplates, and win/loss interviews with other salespeople. The point is to make your company look like the knowledge it produces, not the departments that produce the knowledge. You must decide where it makes sense to begin. If you pick some satellites and end up changing the mix later because others in the company have found your project useful and wish to improve it, so much the better.

Things to Consider

- Focus on content, not on departments.
- Rely on the knowledge storyboard to help you start testing your high-level categories.
- Group low levels of information into subcategories such as competitive intelligence, regulatory standards, and product positioning.
- Each satellite should be a "manageable" domain for a single person who can oversee the content.

Steps to Get You There

1. Take your knowledge storyboard and associate each of the content items with a content center.
2. Make logical groupings within each content center.
3. Refine the subcategories until you've got a manageable picture.

CASE

IN POINT

In a typical product center, content satellites might include information that helps your compliance experts determine if they are meeting statutory requirements. The satellites could include ISO 9000 standards, scientific research, regulatory information, parts lists, etc. In a product center, you also might find user manuals, product availability schedules, and spec sheets. If your product is particularly complex and customizable—such as enterprise software—a product center might include information that helps others make critical implementation decisions. This kind of information would include case studies, performance reports, technology primers, and the like.

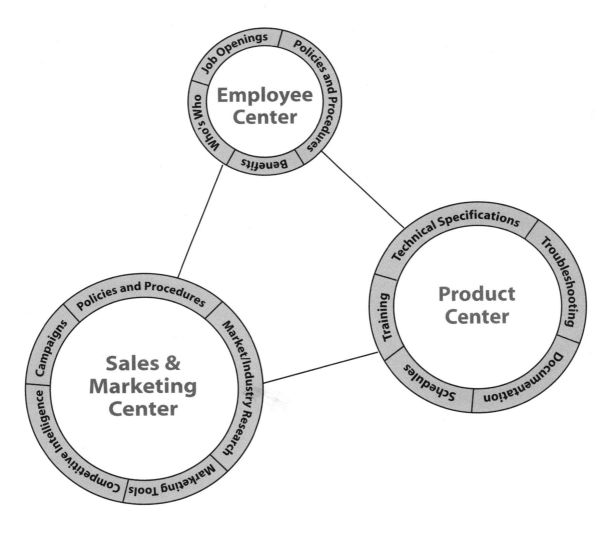

Figure 4.2 Content Satellites

Staffing and Assigning Ownership

Purpose:

Assign ownership to the satellite centers.

Without ownership at the content satellite level, you have no way of enforcing discipline in terms of ensuring the quality of information.

Why Is This Important?

The final step in your knowledge network diagram is assigning ownership of the information and knowledge you have identified. This is where you start to bring the hierarchical structure of your organization into play, combining it with the new knowledge structure you are creating. The objective here is to write in names over each satellite (Figure 4.3).

Owners of information at the satellite level should be management people. This is essential for furthering organizational change, as well as ensuring that staff members keep online (as well as traditional) information up to date and accurate. They need to hold people accountable to the knowledge network. More important, announcing ownership is a key principle of KM: furthering "connection between people" over "mere collections of information." No matter how good your collection and presentation of useful information is, people also need to know who they can call or e-mail for more.

Things to Consider

- Owners of information should be management-level people.
- Owners provide contact points for clarification and validation of content.
- Without ownership at the content satellite level, you have no way of enforcing discipline in terms of ensuring the quality of information.

Steps to Get You There

1. Identify managers for each satellite knowledge center.
2. Put the manager's and author's names at the top of every online document and Web page.
3. Hot link those names to their e-mail addresses.

IN POINT

At J.D. Edwards, we made sure every Web page in the Knowledge Garden had both an owner's name and the page developer's name right at the top. This provides users with points of contact for any content on any single page. This allows users to verify information, as well as check on its accuracy, by contacting a human being on the other end. The point is that no document should be checked in without a contact point that allows users to gain additional information.

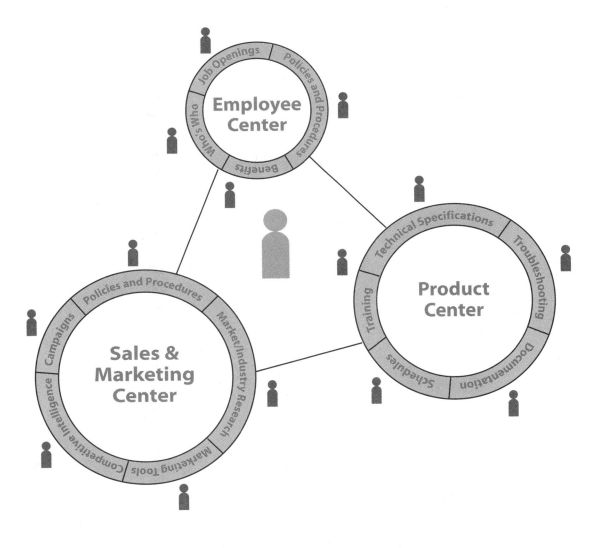

Figure 4.3 Assigning Ownership

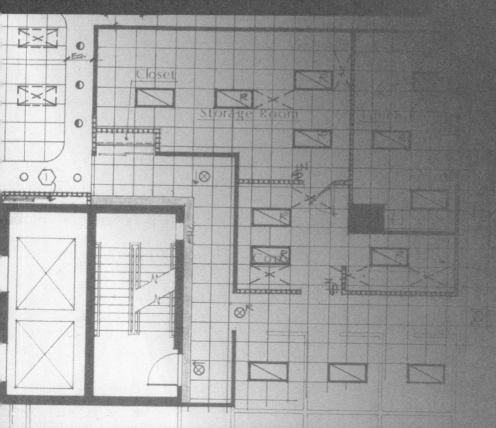

Part Three

Knowledge Architecture

The knowledge architecture identifies the scope of the investment that will be made in managing knowledge. More than a technical solution, it encompasses three components:

- **People**
- **Content**
- **Technology**

A knowledge architecture brings these components together into a powerful working relationship. Here we provide techniques for building road maps to finding important content. We provide job descriptions for people who will supply the content to your organization, and we help you determine relevant technologies for KM. Building your knowledge architecture means assessing your information, then putting people and technology in place to support the management of that information.

The greatest challenge for the Information Age manager is to create an organization that can share knowledge.

—**Thomas A. Stewart,**
Intellectual Capital:
The New Wealth of Organizations

Hiring People

To support a true enterprise-wide knowledge architecture, you'll need to invent new positions and an operation that can spearhead cultural change and help your hierarchical organization adapt to a new knowledge structure. In this chapter, we detail the positions and attendant job descriptions you may draw on when assembling your own company's knowledge architecture. You can use them as they are, or modify them to fit your situation and your budget. At minimum, you'll need people to fill these roles. This may not necessarily involve going out and hiring a whole new set of employees. To get started, you can "re-purpose" existing job functions.

The Levels of Knowledge Managers

The effort to build a knowledge architecture will be undertaken differently by different-sized organizations. A large, enterprise initiative demands dedicated personnel; smaller companies might opt to fold the responsibilities described below into existing job functions. People and departments you may have today that contain the necessary competencies include:

- **Writers**
- **Communications professionals**
- **Web developers**
- **Human resource professionals**
- **Information technology professionals**
- **Graphic artists**
- **Public relations professionals**
- **Competitive intelligence professionals**

Many of these positions already require the necessary skills we're discussing in this chapter. Over time, however, increasing demands placed on these people will make the part-time approach somewhat

To get started, you can "re-purpose" existing job functions.

untenable. Also, don't expect the IT or management information systems professionals alone to have all the right answers. You need content experts in addition to technical experts.

How many people make an effective, beginning team? On the *content* side, the descriptions below dictate four full-time staff members. In an enterprise-wide undertaking, this would probably be the minimum number needed to get started with the right mix of Web, communications, creative, and management skills. Our

Chief Knowledge Officer (CKO)/ Chief Learning Officer (CLO) Job Description

The CKO or CLO is the change agent who markets the importance of knowledge inside the company and enables a global audience to take advantage of it. The CKO ensures that the knowledge architecture is funded, designed, built, and administered. This is not delving into techno-minutiae best left to the CIO—databases, networks, mail, document management, and enterprise resource planning; rather, it is leveraging IT's work in building the infrastructure for the knowledge architecture. The CKO, together with the CIO, drives synergy between work processes and computing processes, making the enterprise more responsive to new business opportunities and changing markets. If one individual fulfills both roles, so much the better.

A CKO's responsibilities are to:
• Determine the structure of enterprise intellectual capital in light of strategic corporate goals.
• Put in place the organization that will manage knowledge that satisfies customers, increases profits, and decreases costs.
• Multiply the value of knowledge.
• Create a successful KM infrastructure in the face of technical, cultural, and logistical barriers.
• Know what information is essential to different people's success.
• Mobilize resources (technology, training, support services) to make sure people have the knowledge they need to succeed.
• Identify high-priority content.
• Capture and manipulate it.
• Distribute it, employing personalization techniques that meet the needs of communities of interest within and across organizational boundaries.

CKO

experience dictates that ultimately 1% of your total personnel should be dedicated to building and maintaining content. On the *technical* side, the goal is to ensure that most IT projects are contributing to the knowledge architecture, rather than being "one-offs" that aren't integrated with each other. You may have to add technical people or hire consultants, depending on the scope of your efforts.

The KM team (Figure 5.1) is a distributed organization that is responsible for translating the department hierarchy of a company into the knowledge chart that we discussed in Chapter Four. It consists of a core team:

Figure 5.1 The Knowledge Management Team

Knowledge Officer

High-level executive who sets the strategic directions for how knowledge will be captured, stored, and delivered. Identifies the key ILPs based on LRP goals and other corporate-level imperatives and objectives. The chief knowledge officer (CKO), if you appoint one.

Knowledge Analyst

Individual charged with the specific knowledge-packaging efforts based on the strategic direction set by the knowledge officer. Identifies the key players and their information needs for critical ILPs.

Knowledge Author

Front-line provider of information. Handles the day-to-day publishing as well as monitoring of information in their particular areas of expertise.

This team is the driving force behind the knowledge strategy of the enterprise. They execute the knowledge audit, handle profiling, evaluate and recommend technology solutions, define corporate-wide common vocabulary, and, working with many others, are ultimately responsible for the accuracy and timeliness of content on the Intranet, Extranet, and Internet.

Knowledge Analyst

The *knowledge analyst* is the first position developed within the company that is aligned with a *knowledge structure* rather than a *departmental structure*. That is, once you envision the company in terms of its content rather than its departmental structure (using the knowledge network map), you can begin to place individuals in appropriate positions. The challenge is in overlaying the knowledge structure on the departmental structure, combining the best of your hierarchy with the new networked form of organization. It's most effective to have this structure in place before, or during, the construction of the technical aspects of your knowledge architecture.

Specifically, the knowledge analyst assesses the critical information needs of key end-users and assembles resources to meet these needs. This involves close work with the user community to determine how internal and external Webs might assist in addressing their needs. The knowledge analyst translates these needs into system requirements and design specifications, and he or she manages the design, development, and implementation of these solutions.

Knowledge Author

The *knowledge author* handles the day-to-day business of publishing information—on a Web server or by means of

Knowledge Analyst Job Responsibilities

- Assume overall responsibility for ensuring users' easy access to information that is useful to them.
- Develop end-user profiles to determine critical information needs.
- Develop conceptual designs based on end-user profiles and work with Internet team, IT, and MIS to translate them into technical realities.
- Work with cross-functional teams to plan and implement KM strategies and specific projects that support overall corporate goals, including corporate vocabulary,

publishing and editorial processes, and user profiles.
- Manage multiple projects from conception to completion.
- Communicate plans, status, and issues to higher levels of management and get their "buy-in."
- Liaise among Internet team, content/editorial specialists, and end-users to ensure that content is updated and available.
- Enforce vocabulary and information design standards across functional areas.

Knowledge Analyst

Knowledge Author Job Responsibilities

- Develop accurate and well-designed Web pages to be delivered by means of Internet, Intranet, or Extranet.
- Provide technical support of Website, incorporating library administration functions such as cataloging information, managing links for effective access to knowledge assets, and managing a basic document management/archive system.

- Tag all documents with appropriate metadata to ensure proper categorization of all documents in the Website.
- Initiate action plans for continual improvement of content and quality of services.
- Understand the information being presented and the needs of the audience in order to provide support for inquiries pertaining to all data on site.

other communications vehicles. This person works with the knowledge analyst to deliver current and accurate information to a specialized audience. She or he is responsible for developing Web-deployed content implementations, maintaining accuracy, and providing expertise in the information that is presented.

In general, a knowledge analyst can support up to ten knowledge authors. But the important thing to remember is that no knowledge author should be independent of a knowledge analyst. The analyst is the one who is responsible for the implementation of the knowledge architecture for a particular content center. The knowledge author produces the content within individual content satellites.

Extended Team

In addition to the new positions outlined on the previous pages, you'll need some other skill sets to support the rollout, design, and maintenance of your Intranet. While the KM team focuses on content, the personnel discussed below center on the more technical aspects of the knowledge architecture.

Technology Support Consultant

This person provides the technical leadership for the knowledge analysts throughout the company, interacting with and coordinating the activities of a cross-functional team including editors, marketers, content contributors, Web server administrators, and the Webmaster. He or she is responsible for

Normal business is about products, services, and the exchange of cash. But in an economy where knowledge and information directly improve the bottom line, personal relationships become much more important.

—**Peter Schwartz**
The Art of the Long View

developing Web-deployed content implementations, providing expertise in the use of KM software, and conducting training on Internet technology.

Interface Design Director

The design director provides specialty consulting and development for Intranet/ Internet knowledge delivery media. He or she is responsible for all functions of information design, site architecture, interface design, multimedia design, and graphics for Internet-related applications.

Multimedia Producer

This person or group develops, directs, and researches Internet multimedia applications, including animation, voice, video, and/or real-time communications over the Intranet, Extranet, and Internet. Multimedia producers also provide consulting expertise in the use of related authoring tools and technology. They must also coordinate network infrastructure and all necessary support to ensure successful implementation of these applications. ◎

Hire dedicated personnel to better manage your intellectual assets. Can you afford *not* to do it? How efficient do you think you'll be in four years if you don't start now? Traditional accounting practices cannot readily value intangibles such as knowledge. Microsoft owns little in the way of tangible assets, yet Microsoft's market capitalization is nearly twice that of General Motors with all its factories and tools. It's knowledge that matters here. Some companies now measure the value of better sharing of knowledge by attempting to quantify:

- **The number of solutions provided online**
- **User sessions on Websites**
- **Time saved hunting for information**
- **Reduced phone calls to help desk**
- **Are customers better served?**
- **Are we doing more with the same number of people?**
- **Are sales cycles shortening?**
- **Are new employees coming up to speed faster?**
- **Is the culture stronger?**

If you looked at the collection of all the documents in the firm, what would it mean to unleash that knowledge that lies as much between documents as within a document?

—**John Seeley Brown,
Xerox Chief Scientist**

Chapter Six

Mobilizing Content

The knowledge storyboard helps you identify the important pieces of information that you need to capture and deliver to your key knowledge workers. The knowledge network diagram helps you locate that information within your departmental structure. In this chapter, we'll take the next step in building your content portfolio: creating a common vocabulary and well-defined content types. Both of these concepts govern the *mobility* of knowledge throughout the extended enterprise—that is, how information is captured, stored, and delivered from sources to users.

The key to successful content mobilization is implementing both of these schemas with discipline. A common vocabulary ensures that a *shared classification scheme* is in effect across your company's different information repositories—whether structured, unstructured, or tacit. Consistent, well-defined content

types provide coherence and structure to the *form of information*. This chapter discusses both concepts in detail and shows you how to implement them effectively.

Avoiding the "Index Everything" Fallacy

Knowledge management does not mean buying a search engine and indexing every document you have on every file server in the company. The results will not be effective enough to justify the investment and effort. The problem with indexing everything is that the search engines on which this strategy is based are designed to deliver hundreds and thousands of hits. It's a research model, not a focused knowledge delivery model based on business needs. In fact, buying a search engine and indexing every bit and byte of information in your existing systems will only increase the InfoSmog in your company.

To avoid the "index everything" fallacy, you need to devise a *common vocabulary*. Also referred to as a "site vocabulary," "metadata," "lexicon," "attributes," or the "bits about bits," this vocabulary is the basis for moving content from sources to users. We cannot overemphasize this point: *One of the very early steps you need to take is establishing the common terms that will be used across all the content in all the repositories you are seeking to manage.*

The common vocabulary is critical to starting small but thinking big. It will allow you to integrate various repositories as you move forward. This is not merely an academic exercise. Without a common understanding of what your products are or what a "white paper" is, you'll produce more InfoSmog. Remember that the common vocabulary is the glue that holds together related pieces of content that may be owned and produced by different groups.

For instance, if product development and customer support have two different understandings of what your products are, it will be very difficult for troubleshooting information to make it back into the product development cycle. It will be cumbersome for a field service rep to gather design information and repair documents at one time. At the very least, communications across those departments will be awkward and unmanageable. Getting them to agree on a common vocabulary is essential, although it also may be very political. Nevertheless, you cannot go very far forward in any KM project without this agreement. Without it, you will definitely end up with a disjointed series of projects that won't ever add up to a bigger picture.

Common Vocabulary

Does your company have a common understanding of what its *products* are? Is your product a service, or is your service a product? Or is this issue open to debate? Do you know what the difference is between an alliance and a partner? Is there a difference? How many different ways does your organization use the term "white paper"? Without a common understanding of terms such as these, how can you expect to make information accessible to any employee, not to mention your key revenue drivers?

metadata

site vocabulary

attributes

lexicon

bits about bits

Setting up a common vocabulary is to begin managing the way your audience submits, searches for, and thinks about the information the company makes available. Every company has its own unique lexicon depending on its industry, culture, and location. Airlines use aviation terms such as "yield management," "contract of carriage," and "passenger seat miles." Enterprise software providers use terms such as "platform," "scalability," and "client/server."

You need to invest significant time and effort in developing a common vocabulary that all departments buy into. For instance, if different departments have different ways of classifying similar information, someone looking for that information will have to know the different departments' schemas in order to retrieve effectively what he or she needs. Instead, a common vocabulary structure will allow someone to search across different information repositories with a single query.

For example, in many companies, products have different names depending on which department you are talking to. Finding marketing information and technical documentation on a particular product should not require you to know

Typical Vocabulary Tags: product version author industry

One of the very early steps you need to take is establishing the common terms that will be used across all the content in all the repositories you are seeking to manage.

two different product names—Marketing's version and Documentation's version. Further, documents are notoriously difficult to classify. A product development white paper is not the same thing as a marketing white paper. To make information easier to find—and therefore more *mobile*—the knowledge manager needs to help set up a common vocabulary across the company.

A common vocabulary structure allows employees to search accurately across many sources of information with a single query.

Common Ground

Putting thought into your common vocabulary from the start will help ensure that your content portfolio is useful, well organized, and easily searched. Essentially, the common vocabulary is a catalog of terms that you use to submit documents to your many different repositories. These terms enable your search engine and personalization delivery systems to grasp content relevant to your users' profiles, preferences, and desired searches.

We don't mean that all departments have to share a single, inflexible schema. Rather, you'll need to tailor your vocabulary for each content center and its attendant satellites. We say "consistent" only to emphasize the high-level categories. Each department should adopt these terms when appropriate, while continuing to use their own classification schemes for specialized information and knowledge.

As a KM team, you need to help different departments develop their own classification systems that address their particular information types. For instance, information that helps you sell products will more often than not be different in

kind from that which helps you support products. However, the product classifications should be common to both marketing and customer service.

Content Types

A common vocabulary is one side of the "mobility" equation for content. The other side is a disciplined use of *content types*. By this, we don't mean "file types"—.pdf, .doc, .xls. We mean defining the kinds of documents you will use to move information throughout your extended enterprise, and then enforcing that structure where and when appropriate. Doing so will reduce the "noise" in your communications strategy and simplify the passing of information from creators to users.

Think about content types as literary "genres." We all know that reading a collection of sonnets will require a different level of attention than reading a John Grisham legal thriller. Why? Because they have different types of content and contain different kinds of information. On the contrary, the use of the term "white paper" generally means "longer than a brochure but not as long as a technical

One important job of the KM team is to establish the common terminology used across the organization.

manual." There are many stages in between, and your KM initiative will benefit from defining what content types are necessary to move information to the right audiences with the appropriate level of detail.

To clarify further, think about how magazines and newspapers have adopted this structure. *The Economist*, for instance, has a reputation for being a comprehensive and trustworthy source of global news. Its loyal readers know that each issue will contain specific kinds of articles: "Politics This Week" and "Business This Week" provide highly distilled summaries of world news; "Science and Technology" and "Finance and Economics" provide more detailed discussions on particular issues in these areas. As a reader, I know what level of detail each of these contains and whether or not I'm part of the intended audience.

Newspapers have capitalized on this mode of organization as well. Any given newspaper's information is always different from day to day, but the sections remain the same. You can count on the *Wall Street Journal*'s three main sections. When you want mutual fund price/performance information, you turn to "Money and Investing," not "Marketplace." You do this because you know what kind of information is contained in each section. Navigation is simplified through a predictable structure.

Maintaining Discipline

Looking at the knowledge storyboard, you can see the information that makes up the core of your content portfolio. This map does not tell you, however, what *form* this information should take. Content types give formal structure to your company's information.

Remember, the purpose of using well-disciplined content types is to introduce simplicity and predictability into how your company mobilizes information. Look at each piece of information listed on the knowledge storyboard and think about each in terms of complexity. The more complex information will require more sophisticated content types. Don't narrow your focus to text-based documents. A document may be a particular view into a database, a computer-based training module, an instructional video, etc.

In most cases, you'll define your content types in terms of three issues:

- **Ownership**
- **Level of detail**
- **Appropriate audience**

Focusing on these issues will help you simplify the movement of information among your key revenue drivers. They will know which documents are appropriate to their own information and learning needs. They won't have to waste time figuring out if a particular document is relevant to them.

Assigning Ownership

Ownership is critical to implementation of content types. Very often, departments enter into "turf battles" regarding the kinds of information they own. Product Development often butts up against Marketing. In many companies, they frequently squabble over how to position product features and functions in the marketplace. To focus each department on its particular area of expertise, you'll need to assign departmental ownership to each content type (Figure 6.1). You can start at a high level and work from there:

- **Product Development owns the "what" and "when" information—what a product can and can't do and when it will be available.**
- **Marketing owns the "why" and "who" information—why someone would want to purchase the product and who are its likely buyers.**
- **Training owns the "how" information—how to use the product.**

From this starting point, you can unfold each of these types of content in greater detail. "What" and "when" might include "vision" statements, functionality schedules, product design plans, and technical specifications. "Why" and "who" information might include product positioning statements, customer profiles, brochures, and press releases. "How" information usually encompasses user manuals, instructional videos, and computer-based training modules.

In some cases, ownership may be cooperative. Marketing and Product Development may agree to joint ownership of vision statements and product design plans based on perceived market demand. The point is to make sure that each content type is clearly defined in terms of audience, level of detail, and ownership. This approach will simplify your communications plan and make information more mobile across your enterprise. ◎

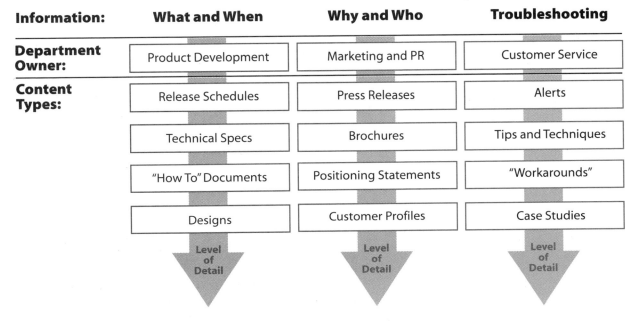

	What and When	**Why and Who**	**Troubleshooting**
Information:			
Department Owner:	Product Development	Marketing and PR	Customer Service
Content Types:	Release Schedules	Press Releases	Alerts
	Technical Specs	Brochures	Tips and Techniques
	"How To" Documents	Positioning Statements	"Workarounds"
	Designs	Customer Profiles	Case Studies
	Level of Detail	Level of Detail	Level of Detail

Figure 6.1 Well-Defined Content Types Give Formal Structure to Your Company's Information

Because of the maturity of technology standards, it is now possible to plan an enterprise architecture rather than just adding another room to the farmhouse.

—Don Tapscott,
*The Digital Economy:
Promise and Peril in the Age of
Networked Intelligence*

Chapter Seven

Building The Technical Architecture

This chapter shows you how to build on your company's existing network assets and improve them to better enable content management. If your organization does not have a network, it seems unlikely that you would have read this far. (And this chapter won't be of much use to you.) You may be considering outsourcing the hosting of an Intranet for cost reasons. Outsourcing of Intranets seems an intriguing possibility for reducing costs and headaches, letting companies concentrate on content and not technology. But in 1998, we are not aware of any sizable company that has begun doing this, because of unsatisfactory security and, perhaps, political concerns.

We are less concerned with bits and bytes here; this is more about building up your network to accommodate more effective knowledge sharing. This chapter does not focus on a specific product or technology; rather, it sketches out the framework for knowledge-related technology purchase and deployment decision-making, since there is no one single technology that does enterprise KM.

Keep in mind that while we outline for you the range of technologies you'll want to consider, don't feel that you have to begin by purchasing all this software and paying the consulting fees that come with installing it. In fact, it's unlikely that any company would have the bandwidth to purchase and deploy all the things listed below at one time. It's more realistic to take an iterative approach. Where budgeting is tight, it would be entirely appropriate to begin by using the principles in this book to simply organize your most vital information better and deliver it through simple (and cheap) Web pages on your internal Website (or your public Website, for that

Technology enables delivery; people enable information; and information, when action is taken on it, enables knowledge.

matter, if security isn't a concern.) This alone could be a huge win for your organization if you're just starting out.

Your organization is a knowledge network. It always has been, of course, but the challenge posed by the growth of the knowledge economy is to make employees and customer relationships more efficient and to drive more revenue for your business by making better use of the knowledge you have. Technology enables delivery; people enable information; and information, when action is taken on it, enables knowledge.

A knowledge *architecture*, once in place, is a federation of technologies running on top of your existing network. You may think of these components as layers of technology. When laid on top of each other, they form a cohesive technical foundation for others to tap into like a power strip (Figure 7.1).

Overview

The first layer is the access layer (security, membership, or authentication)—the gateway to information within your organization.

The interface (usually the browser) is the second layer, presenting simplicity to the user. This component masks the complexity of your networked organization and the underlying processes used to deliver information. The interface provides a universal view to documents, e-mail, calendars, people, etc.

The third layer is "intelligence"—products and programming that provide filtering of information, search across many repositories, personalization, and agents who know and act on user preferences.

The fourth layer comprises the many applications that provide the "value-add" or "show-me" layer. These applications and technologies provide users with productivity enhancements and improved ways of doing their jobs. This layer includes authoring and publishing tools, site analysis tools, document management, discussion databases, competitive intelligence knowledge bases, calendars, employee yellow pages, Website analysis tools, sales force automation, and executive "balanced scorecard" applications.

The transport or network layer is made up of your Intranet Web deployment, e-mail, streaming technologies, and collaborative tools.

The sixth layer consists of repositories: data warehouses, legacy systems, document repositories, and more.

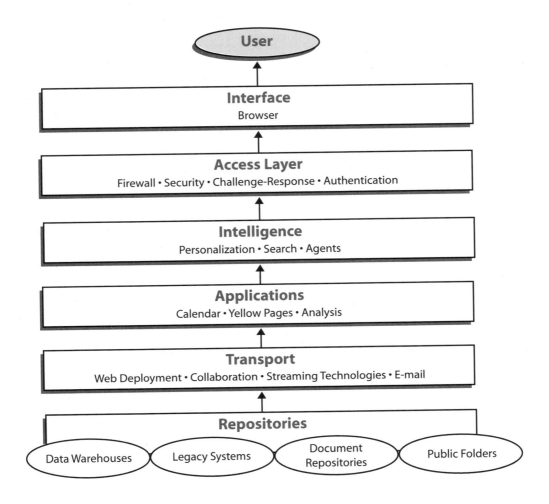

Figure 7.1 Layers of the Technical Architecture

Access

Purpose:

Information Protection and Security

Why Is This Important?

Your company is a knowledge network where the boundaries are being redrawn (Figure 7.2). Org charts, department walls, and cubicle walls have been replaced by firewalls, time zones, and competing technologies. Your employees, suppliers, business partners, and customers and their hunger for information transcend the physical boundaries of the organization. The demands for product information, support resources, market intelligence, and lessons learned about new products are mounting. The traditional security model breaks down while "wide-open access" is not acceptable to corporate counsel.

To strike a reasonable balance, your policies for access and the technical architecture must meet demands for access to information while balancing legal and information security concerns.

Things to Consider

- Access to information is based on profiles derived from the knowledge audit (Chapter Two).
- Choose technology for providing access (direct access? virtual private network? NT security? password protection? Extranet? dial-up? dedicated lines?)
- Who will manage security groups, passwords, and sign-ons?

Steps to Get You There

1. Establish a cross-functional team to define access methods based on findings of knowledge audit. The team should consist of IT, legal, and key departmental stakeholders such as marketing, HR, and customer support. Spread accountability, but drive home the importance of closure.

2. Finalize data classification issues and risks. Be crisp here. This will help construct the blueprint for IT. IT will require a well-thought-out business plan.

3. Assess access methods and associated costs. This may impact the way in which you design the architecture. Dial-up vs. virtual private network could impact performance.

4. Determine how network access costs will be passed on to business partners.

5. Market your efforts; communicate your plans to business partners, customers, and employees.

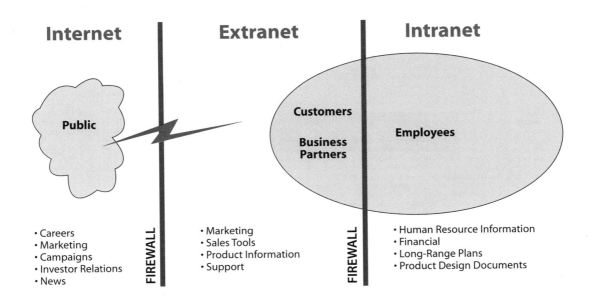

Figure 7.2 Network Access Model

Interface

Purpose:

*Building a Universal View
of the Enterprise*

Why Is This Important?

Now it's time to pave the path for, and eliminate barriers to, information. Think of the interface as an application. You'll make use of icons, tree controls, personalized navigation, and graphic design. You are attempting to build a universal "view" of the enterprise—a window to the repository of "truths" about your organization, products, and customers (Figure 7.3). Do your interface design well and you will increase your effectiveness tenfold.

Things to Consider

- Provide universal access to disparate sources, including structured, unstructured, and tacit knowledge.
- Simplify the view of the universe of available knowledge.
- Establish personalized, uniform, and consistent navigation.

Steps to Get You There

1. Hire a talented, dedicated interface designer.
2. Determine early if the interface will be browser-based or an alternative client-side application.
3. Factor in usability testing and scalability.
4. Work with your IT organization (MIS) to design tree controls and icons.
5. Understand the underlying applications, search, and results. Knowing the format in which information will be presented will help immensely in the design.

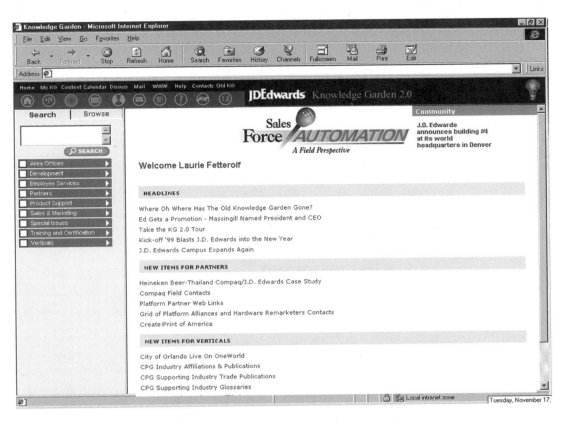

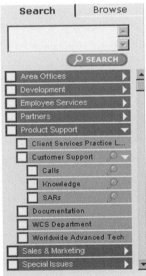

Figure 7.3 Personalized Home Page, Search Tool, and Navigational Buttons

Intelligence

Purpose:

Personalized Experience

with Information

Why Is This Important?

The intelligence layer makes personalization possible. It cuts through InfoSmog and reduces the time spent hunting for information. This layer consists of the following elements:

Registration of users in a membership directory provides the most efficient method for presenting tailored information to your audience. The combination of a well-managed membership directory, a robust editorial process, profiles of core competencies, subscriptions, e-mail, and usage analysis comes together to present simplicity through the browser. Users see a selection of content pulling from a variety of updated, relevant sources. You are customizing the presentation of information based on users' needs (Figure 7.4).

Subscription allows users to subscribe to different kinds of information—sales/promotional, customer support, FDA regulations, etc. New information submitted to these categories (including subcategories) is pushed to the users' desktops based on his or her subscriptions. Subscriptions should be based on user selections as well as users' profiles and job descriptions.

Today's **search engines** are built on the Web model of "indexing everything." This is a research model for finding information, whereas many corporate Intranet users are engaged in business reference searches. Returning 500 hits is acceptable for researchers using the World Wide Web, but it is not acceptable to the majority of users of Intranets. If you think managing knowledge begins and ends with a search engine, read on. Search, as with any of the components in this book, is but one of many pieces of this puzzle. Search technology is important, but it should supplement the federated technology approach, not serve as a "silver bullet" for your efforts.

Steps to Get You There

Registration

1. Leverage the resources you worked with in establishing the access model.
2. The team should consist of IT, legal, and key departmental stakeholders such as HR, and customer support. Spread accountability, but drive home the importance of closure.
3. Establish profiles based on relationships, roles, and competencies.
4. Build catalogs that contain information relative to the profiles established.

Subscription

1. Establish specific information sharing with business partners and field employees.
2. Consider methods for change notification (e-mail, personalization).

3. Allow end-users the ability to subscribe to information collections such as press releases, schedules, documentation, HR info, and product updates.
4. Launch and expire content automatically.
5. Control assets including multiple content types.

Search

1. Full text search—users can search for words or phrases in the full text of documents.
2. A single query finds information, regardless of where it is stored.
3. Add metadata information to documents to enable more precise searching.
4. Users will see only the result set for documents to which they have access.

Things to Consider

- Registration
- Subscription
- Search

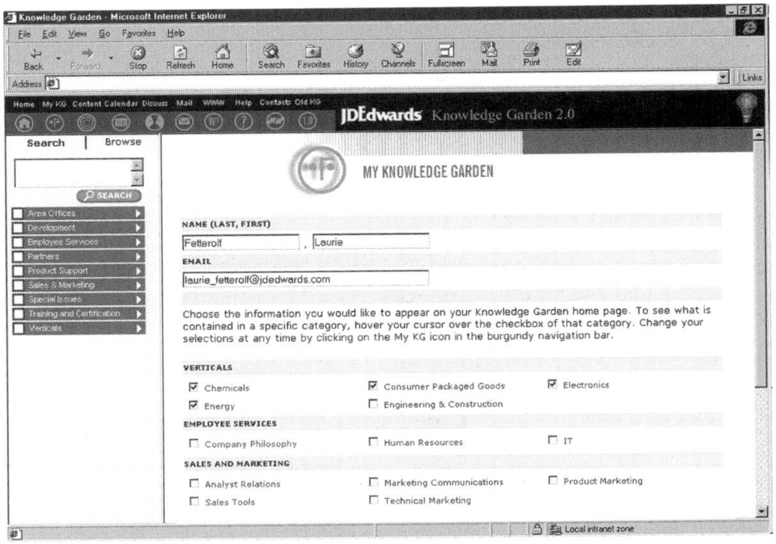

Figure 7.4 Knowledge Garden's Registration Page

This screen is reproduced by permission of J.D. Edwards World Solutions. Copyright, J.D. Edwards, 1998. J.D. Edwards is a registered trademark in the U.S. and/or other countries.

Knowledge-Enabling Applications

Purpose:

Creating a Competitive Edge

Why Is This Important?

Knowledge-enabling applications are the applications that come together to provide the "value-add" or "show-me" layer (Figure 7.5). They provide users with productivity enhancements and improved ways of doing their jobs. This layer includes authoring and publishing tools, site analysis tools, document management, discussion databases, competitive intelligence knowledge bases, calendars, employee yellow pages, Website analysis tools, sales force automation, and executive "balanced scorecard" applications.

The list of applications provides a framework for you to get started. This is "where the rubber meets the road" in KM; infrastructure is a commodity, and the network is a given. Now you must leverage your infrastructure to create a competitive edge for your organization.

While creativity could expand this list a hundredfold, we have chosen a handful of applications that will allow you to get started and begin to show value relatively quickly.

Analysis

Companies are using sophisticated measures to try to show the value of sharing knowledge better. While difficult to measure directly, you can tie knowledge sharing to other measures to try to get at the impact you are having. Website statistical analysis tools are certainly one method of determining what people are interested in requesting from a Website; whether they get what they are looking for is open to interpretation, but this information is helpful in terms of improving information design.

Things to Consider

- Document management/ imaging
- Decision support
- Collaborative tools
- Data management
- Sales force automation

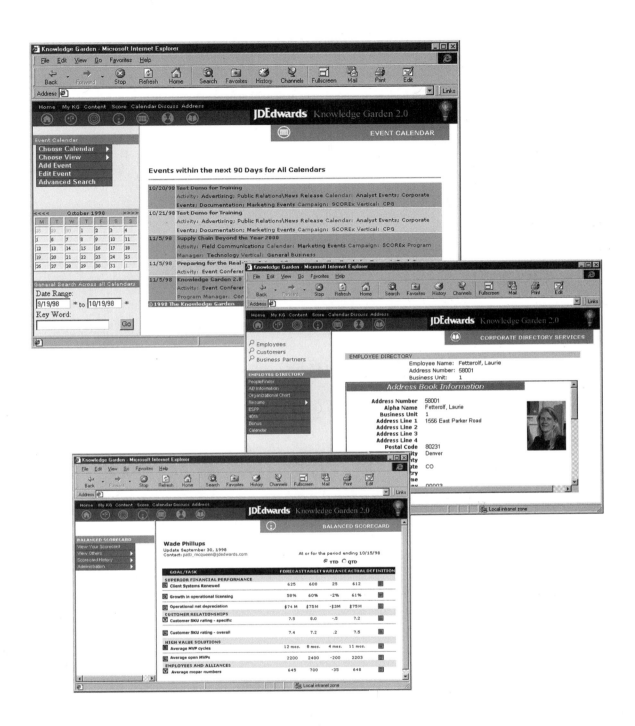

Figure 7.5 Knowledge Garden Application Samples

Transport

Purpose:

Network Connectivity

and Data Transport

Why Is This Important?

In order to implement a knowledge architecture across your enterprise, you will continually re-evaluate your existing technical network. Your company has become a network of relationships (Figure 7.6). You have moved from a concern for transporting transactional data and accounting transactions to a concern for transporting intellectual assets (knowledge) across the network to the right people at the right time. Today, your network may be moving e-mail, documents, video and audio clips, news, and many other types of content— or it may not.

We look to the network backbone to provide traditional connectivity across the LAN, WAN, and Intra/Extra/Internet, and now, to support the collection, organization, and sharing of information.

Collaborative tools provide an economical way to bring expertise and knowledge to bear on a specific problem or situation, at a specific point in time.

People have been collaborating for a long time, of course, by using e-mail and the telephone. In aircraft cockpits and hospital emergency rooms, collaboration has been a matter of life or death for years. There's nothing new here for business, except perhaps some technological twists that can improve retention and sharing of solutions developed in previous situations.

Things to Consider

- Network traffic
- Impact of video conferencing
- Bandwidth issues related to streaming of Web-based training modules, audio, and video
- Connectivity speeds (keep offline users in mind when designing)
- Open systems that support streaming, HTML, scripting, URLs, graphics, and multimedia
- Search tool that can search forums
- Ability to allow for live presentations and moderated events

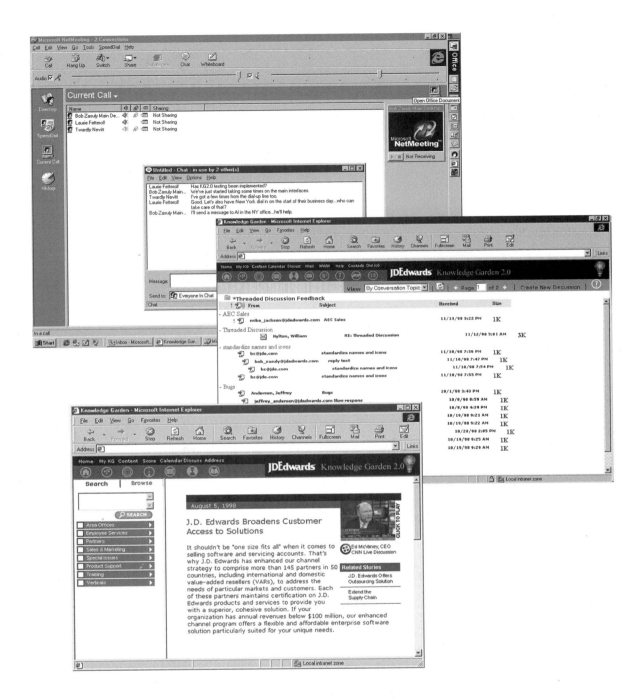

Figure 7.6 Collaboration Tools May Include Microsoft NetMeeting, Discussion Groups, and Microsoft NetShow

Repositories

Purpose:

Storage

Why Is This Important?

The technical architecture we've been describing should result now in your attacking the integration of loosely connected systems, databases, and file systems. It is likely that you'll be faced with mining information from legacy sources, as well as those "fresh" data sources cropping up throughout the organization today (Figure 7.7).

This is potentially a large project. You may want to consider a full-time data architect to help you here. To save time and be assured of moving forward, focus your efforts on "controlled" sources of information, those having KAs, editors, or administrators that are in charge of the data, as opposed to uncontrolled public file servers hosting thousands of publicly shared, but uncataloged, documents. In such a case, you may want to include information only in certain directories or, alternatively, assign ownership to an individual KA.

Things to Consider

- Inventory data sources (see our discussion of the knowledge audit in Chapter One).
- Do you have controlled rather than uncontrolled sources of information? Be selective.
- Architect database schema that allows easy extraction of fields in database.
- Single-source repositories.

Steps to Get You There

1. Employ the services of a data architect.
2. Establish schema (architecture) that integrates with access model.
3. Create data architecture based on integration of disparate sources.

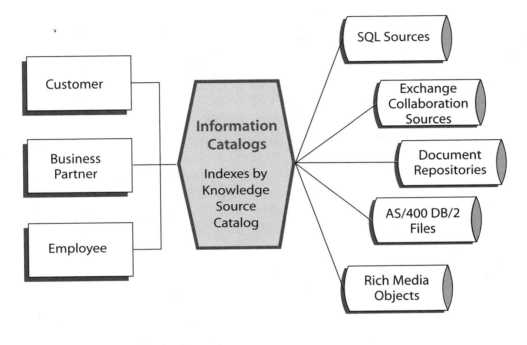

Figure 7.7 Repositories of Information

Part Four

The Ninety-Day Action Plan

In the first 90 days, you need to think big, start small, and deliver quickly. You have to focus on a single job function or a single ILP and build a solution. This doesn't have to be a complete solution, but a demonstration version that will help you sell Web-based KM as a valuable undertaking. We can't overemphasize this point: don't try to take on everything at once. Starting small is the best way to prove that you can complete a KM project that delivers measurable value. A successful initial project can become the basis for further projects as you build momentum toward the "big picture."

Ninety-Day Checklist
- **Choose a single business cycle that you can improve**
- **Begin the knowledge audit**
- **Begin building your core team**
- **Choose your technology**
- **Market your efforts**
- **Maintain your content**

Day 1–Day 30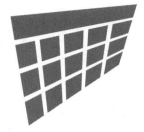

❏ Choose a single business cycle that you can improve

❏ Begin the knowledge audit

pick up an issue that u think can be improved

Choose a single business cycle that you can improve

Before you begin buying Web servers, search engines, or document management systems, you need to determine the immediate purposes for your initiatives. What business cycles can you positively influence by delivering data, information, and knowledge more effectively? You may focus on speeding up the assimilation of partners into your processes, or you may decide that delivering competitive intelligence to sales reps can help you compress the sales cycle. The point is to pick a definable issue and focus on improving it with better content delivery.

Begin the knowledge audit

Once you've chosen the particular business cycle that you can positively affect, you need to begin putting together both of the diagrams outlined in Chapters Three and Four: the knowledge storyboard and the knowledge network. Recall that the storyboard involves four steps:

- **Step One: Pick a business cycle or process and understand how it works.**
- **Step Two: Break the cycle down to every event where people need to act.**
- **Step Three: Identify the people who use information at each point.**
- **Step Four: Select the content necessary to act at each ILP.**

The knowledge network diagram requires three steps:

- **Step One: Pick five to eight categories that represent the organizational framework for capturing and delivering information.**
- **Step Two: Break down content centers into lower levels of detail.**
- **Step Three: Assign ownership to the satellite centers.**

Day 31–Day 60

❏ Begin building your core team

❏ Choose your technology

Begin building your core team

Put together a small team first. You can make a great start with only four people: a manager, a KA, a designer, and a Web developer. You may want to consider using a consultant as part of your team. Obviously, the size of the team has to fit the size of the undertaking. Our experience is that 1% of your total employee base is a good long-range size for your extended KM team—including knowledge analysts, knowledge authors, and other positions described in Chapter Five. This 1% encompasses dedicated, full-time people. Our early efforts at J.D. Edwards (4000 employees) began with a core team of four, but quickly grew to eight. Over time, we have found that 40 full-time people are necessary to support adequately our Intranet, Extranet, and external Website. One person alone will have it tough. It is hard to imagine any one person having sufficient editorial, managerial, evangelical, communications, Web, graphical, and technical skills to take on even a pilot project.

Choose your technology

While you are starting small with your demo project, communicate from the outset, with everyone who will listen, that your grand vision for your technology is a *knowledge architecture*. Your project will ultimately become the infrastructure effort that spans the enterprise. This is not another one-off stovepipe effort, like the ones that may currently be underway in many departments in your company. This is a crucial difference, but one that may not be obvious to many people. All current projects should be evaluated soon in light of what you choose as your knowledge architecture with an eye to:

- **Narrowing your technology footprint**
- **Getting the right information to the right people**
- **Providing universal access to everyone**
- **Providing consistent navigation across many applications, documents, and data sources**

Day 61–Day 90

❒ Market your efforts

❒ Maintain your content

Market your efforts

Market your efforts and show people how your solution can help. Use your demo to communicate the benefits of a KM solution and to sell the concept of the knowledge architecture. This is an effective way to build goodwill, further assess what must be done, and understand more clearly your operating environment.

Your first demo may be simple. You don't need anything fancy; perhaps you are just making needed information available from a convenient spot. You are making accessible what was previously scattered or hard to find. This alone could save your company a lot of time and money. It also serves to set the stage for your further efforts.

Maintain your content

Determine how you are going to keep your content updated. This could mean assembling an editorial process that will sustain an online publishing effort, full time. It could be as simple as a one-step approval process, or as complex as an "enterprise broadcast network."

Attempt to keep content fresh, and dig into your hard-to-get-at tacit knowledge using reporters, editors, videographers, and others to interview and capture win/loss information, successful sales and support stories, or experiences valuable to your situation.

Index

Wayne Applehans manages the Knowledge Resource Strategies Group for J.D. Edwards in Denver. His experience spans human resource management, organizational communications, world-wide marketing, and information technology in both the utility and high-tech industries. His ability to blend cultural issues with Web technologies has led to the development of one of today's most successful knowledge management initiatives. With a degree in organizational communications from the University of Colorado, Applehans continues to draw on both his education, HR experience, and technology background to assist organizations in leveraging intellectual capital to sustain a competitive advantage.

Alden Globe, J.D., knowledge architect for J.D. Edwards in Denver, is a Webmaster, writer, and strategist. He has worked with Nestle, Canada Malting, Continental Airlines, numerous "new media" firms, and the State of Connecticut. With degrees in philosophy from the University of Toronto and law from Franklin Pierce Law Center, Globe understands enterprise information initiatives.

Greg Laugero, Ph.D., manages technical publications for J.D. Edwards World Source Company. He brings to businesses an extensive understanding of how to produce, capture, classify, and share information. As a doctoral candidate (English) at the State University of New York at Stony Brook, he studied the history of knowledge in England with emphasis on libraries, the publishing industry, and the emergence of the popular press.

Contact the authors by e-mail at:
wayne_applehans@managingknowledge.com
alden_globe@managingknowledge.com
greg_laugero@managingknowledge.com

Addison-Wesley Computer and Engineering Publishing Group

How to Interact with Us

1. Visit our Web site

http://www.awl.com/cseng

When you think you've read enough, there's always more content for you at Addison-Wesley's web site. Our web site contains a directory of complete product information including:

- Chapters
- Exclusive author interviews
- Links to authors' pages
- Tables of contents
- Source code

You can also discover what tradeshows and conferences Addison-Wesley will be attending, read what others are saying about our titles, and find out where and when you can meet our authors and have them sign your book.

2. Subscribe to Our Email Mailing Lists

Subscribe to our electronic mailing lists and be the first to know when new books are publishing. Here's how it works: Sign up for our electronic mailing at **http://www.awl.com/cseng/mailinglists.html**. Just select the subject areas that interest you and you will receive notification via email when we publish a book in that area.

3. Contact Us via Email

cepubprof@awl.com
Ask general questions about our books.
Sign up for our electronic mailing lists.
Submit corrections for our web site.

bexpress@awl.com
Request an Addison-Wesley catalog.
Get answers to questions regarding
your order or our products.

innovations@awl.com
Request a current Innovations Newsletter.

webmaster@awl.com
Send comments about our web site.

elizabeth.spainhour@awl.com
Submit a book proposal.
Send errata for an Addison-Wesley book.

cepubpublicity@awl.com
Request a review copy for a member of the media
interested in reviewing new Addison-Wesley titles.

We encourage you to patronize the many fine retailers who stock Addison-Wesley titles. Visit our online directory to find stores near you or visit our online store: **http://store.awl.com/** or call **800-824-7799**.

Addison Wesley Longman
Computer and Engineering Publishing Group
One Jacob Way, Reading, Massachusetts 01867 USA
TEL 781-944-3700 • FAX 781-942-3076